LIVING
IN
THE
LIGHT

Leading Youth to Deeper Spirituality

Walt Marcum

ABINGDON PRESS
NASHVILLE

LIVING IN THE LIGHT:
Leading Youth to Deeper Spirituality

Copyright © 1994 by Abingdon Press

This book is printed on acid-free recycled paper.

Library of Congress Cataloging-in-Publication Data

Marcum, Walt
    Living in the light: leading youth to deeper spirituality/
Walt Marcum.
        p.   cm.--(Essentials for Christian youth)
    Includes bibliographical references.
    ISBN **0-687-39235-7** (pbk.: alk. paper)
    1. Church work with youth.   2. Youth–Religious life.   I. Title.
II. Series.
BV4447.M284   1994
259'.23–dc20   94-12860

Quotations are from the New Revised Standard Version Bible, Copyright 1989 by the Division of Christian Education of the National Council of the Churches of Christ in the USA. Used by permission.

Photo Credits:
Jean-Claude Lejeune—pages 4, 10, 18, 27, 34, 39, 45, 48, 82, 90.
Jim Whitmer—pages 51, 60, 64, 71, 76, 88, 99.

94 95 96 97 98 99 00 01 02 03—10 9 8 7 6 5 4 3 2 1

MANUFACTURED IN THE UNITED STATES OF AMERICA

For Melissa

who came into our lives
at the age of four as a gift from God,
and who will soon be teaching me youth ministry

ACKNOWLEDGMENTS

I would like to thank Jill Reddig, Paul Franklyn, Cynthia Gadsden, and Abingdon Press for their encouragement in this project and for their patience and understanding during the extended delay.

A special thanks to the North Texas Conference for allowing me the opportunity to work with youth at the conference and district level; to Perkins School of Youth Ministry, where this material was originally taught; to the Reverend Cammy Gaston, my co-teacher in the spirituality course at Perkins; and to the youth of both Highland Park United Methodist Church and White Rock United Methodist Church in Dallas for giving me the opportunity and privilege of being in ministry with youth.

CONTENTS

INTRODUCTION

Those of us who work with youth have a unique privilege. We work with young people during the crucial years in which their basic faith and commitment to God take form. During the adolescent years we form our worldview, develop our ethical values, decide what we do or do not believe, and acquire the basic shape and content of the faith that will take us through life. As much as we like to talk about dramatic adult conversions in our faith, the reality is that normally, it is during their adolescent years that we either reach or fail to reach people.

This book is designed to be a resource for you in your work with youth. It provides a basic understanding of adolescent spirituality and the basic tools for working with young people.

What Is Spirituality?

Several different understandings of spirituality exist within the Christian community. The definition used in this book focuses on relationship. Our faith calls us into relationship—with God and with others. Behind all of our techniques and activities in spiritual growth, we have one overriding goal and concern: to develop a personal relationship with God through Jesus Christ and our neighbor. The ultimate goal of spiritual growth is nothing less than the fulfillment of Jesus' great Commandment to love God with all our heart, mind, soul, and strength, and our neighbor as ourself. When we study the Bible, pray, worship, or engage in any spiritual exercise, this overriding goal is behind that activity.

Five Characteristics of Contemporary Spirituality

The way Christian spirituality has been expressed has changed over the centuries. In contemporary spirituality there are five fundamental characteristics:

1. **Spirituality is this-worldly rather than otherworldly.** There is no doubt that at times in our history spirituality has focused on escaping the world we live in and

has focused on a world other that this one. In contrast, contemporary spirituality is this-world oriented. Through our spiritual disciplines we develop our relationship with God here and now. We also develop our relationships with those around us. We do not seek to take youth out of the world. Rather, we seek to have young people encounter and experience the living God, who is very much present in our world, and to engage them more fully in this world in which God is at work.

2. **Spirituality is experiential rather than cognitive.** Spirituality has at times been closely identified with the cognitive and the rational. We study; we memorize; we discuss. In short, we approach God and our spirituality much as we would any other topic or subject. The result has been that we sometimes have focused more on learning *about* God than experiencing and developing a relationship *with* God. The spirituality advocated in this book focuses on direct encounter with God and the nurturing of our relationship with God. God is not a topic to be studied. God is a living reality in our midst, which we need to encounter and experience directly. We need a dynamic, living relationship, not just an understanding.

3. **Spirituality is more concerned with relationship than with religion.** At its worst, religion can become a substitute for faith, or even a barrier to faith. Our religious practices can become ends in themselves. A healthy spirituality seeks to develop relationships. Religious practices and activities are merely tools to assist in that goal.

4. **Spirituality is more corporate than private.** Christian spirituality is essentially and fundamentally communal. Relationship requires others. At times it is helpful to pull away to "a place apart," as Jesus did. But this is not the norm. Our faith is lived in the midst of others, not apart from them. Our relationship with God and our experience of God have a strong corporate component. This is especially true for youth.

5. **Spirituality is more positive than negative.** There is an old limerick that expresses a perverted view of spirituality which still plagues the Christian community: "Don't smoke. Don't cuss. Don't chew. Don't mess around with them folk that do." All of us have run into this attitude in one way or another. The danger with this type of thinking is that it implies that we can grow in our faith and our relationship with God simply by avoiding certain things. It is fundamentally negative in its approach.

A healthy spirituality is more positive than negative. While it is true that there are many harmful things we need to avoid, the real focus in spiritual growth is on the positive ways we can develop our relationship with God and make ourselves more open to God.

Three Keys to Spiritual Growth

It would be nice to think that there are some magical short cuts to spirituality. When we are tempted to look for the magic Bible study, prayer activity, or camp experience that somehow will make the youth we work with suddenly more spiritual, it's helpful to remember these three keys to spiritual growth.

1. **Spiritual growth is a process, not an event.** Mountain-top experiences are wonderful, and they can play a key role in our spiritual development. But spiritual

growth itself is a process, not an event. Theologically, spirituality has to do with what the apostle Paul calls "sanctification," or "going on to perfection." Growth involves change. It is dynamic rather than static. And it involves every aspect of our lives, as well as every moment.

2. **Spiritual growth also takes time.** Spirituality deals with the sum total of our spiritual experiences across our entire lives. It can't be rushed. We can't make it happen. We can only provide the opportunities and the openness that enable God to work within us.

3. **Spiritual growth requires discipline.** It is also helpful to remember that spiritual growth does not normally just happen. It has always involved spiritual disciplines—engaging in certain activities to open ourselves up to God's presence in our lives. No one is arguing that God can't work without scripture, prayer, and worship. But it is also true that these disciplines have proved to be valuable tools for countless Christians throughout the ages.

Understanding Adolescent Spirituality

Adolescent spirituality is not fundamentally different from any other spirituality. The difference is that in youth work, our context is the realities and needs of youth. Adolescent spiritual growth is linked to adolescent development. As we grow, more things become possible. We work with young people during the period when they undergo the most profound changes in their lives. Their brains develop; their bodies change; their capacity to think undergoes a dramatic shift; their world broadens. All this affects their spiritual growth.

The teen years provide challenges as well as opportunities. It is challenging because adolescents do not have a fully formed or developed faith. They can be—by definition—immature. They do not have a great depth of experience and understanding to draw on. Adolescence is a time of seeking, searching, questioning, and challenging. Teenagers will critique and test the faith they have inherited from their families and faith community. They are also inconsistent. They conpartmentalize. One minute you believe that a young person—or a group—is on the verge of the kingdom of God. The next minute you believe the opposite.

But the opportunities far outweigh the challenges. Young people are by far the most open to new experiences and activities. They are eager to learn, experience, and grow. They will engage in activities that few adults would even consider. They readily see God and Jesus as friends or buddies. Youth ministry constantly places them in places and situations where great mountain-top experiences happen. And often we are there with them during these moments.

The Youth Worker's Personal Spiritual Development

A word needs to be said about the personal spiritual growth of the adults who work with youth. There is an old truism in the counseling profession: You can't take a counselee further than you are yourself. It's difficult for the person being helped to become healthier than the counselor or therapist he or she works with.

This is true in spiritual growth as well. How can we expect kids to grow in our ministries if we ourselves are not growing spiritually as well? It's not a matter of our being spiritual giants. But it is a matter of our being in a living, dynamic relationship with God. Spiritual growth cannot be reduced to a series of tricks, gimmicks, or activities. Our relationship with God and our relationships with the youth we work with have a direct bearing on our ability to work with them in the area of spiritual growth.

Our most powerful tool in working with youth is our own relationship with God. We need to be actively working to grow in that relationship through Bible study, prayer, worship, and the other disciplines. The youth we work with can sense this in us. If our relationship with God is alive and dynamic, it will show. And the youth we work with will want to experience what we have experienced.

What Is in This Book?

The world probably does not need another book about spiritual growth. There are several good books on adolescent spiritual development currently available, and several others on spiritual growth in youth ministry. This book is a resource manual. It is short on theory and long on practical advice. It is written by a youth worker and draws on more than twenty-five years' experience in working with youth. It also seeks to bring together in one place a lot of practical, proven ideas and techniques from a wide variety of sources.

* **Chapter 1** explores using Bible study with youth as a key to developing a relationship with God. It covers the importance of the Bible for spiritual growth, some basic guidelines for Bible study with youth, and 19 different Bible study techniques that have proven effective in youth ministry.

* **Chapter 2** deals with active prayer (speaking to God). It explores a basic understanding of the nature of prayer, some practical suggestions for prayer with youth, and 24 prayer activities that work well with youth.

* **Chapter 3** deals with a special type of prayer often neglected in contemporary youth ministry—dispositional prayer. It focuses on learning how to listen to God, not just speak to God. This type of prayer is particularly appropriate for youth in developing a relationship with God. After covering the components of dispositional prayer, the remainder of the chapter is devoted to 10 specific dispositional prayer techniques.

* **Chapter 4** explores worship with youth. It includes a definition of worship and the key characteristics of Christian worship. The bulk of the chapter deals with: (1) *involving youth in Sunday morning worship;* (2) *special "Youth Sunday" worship services;* (3) *youth-planned and youth-led worship for Sunday evenings;* (4) *worship on trips and special occasions;* and (5) *forming a youth worship committee.* It also contains several examples of youth-planned and youth-led worship services and devotions.

* **Chapter 5** pulls together a lot of additional or special spiritual growth techniques: spiritual mentoring, journaling, spiritual autobiographies, dreamwork, music, fasting, depth discipleship training, mission and service, using small groups, and the role of moral values and ethical decision-making in spiritual growth.

* **Chapter 6** offers a complete three-day spiritual-life retreat which uses many of the ideas in this book. You may find it helpful to use the retreat as written, to borrow ideas from it, or to use it to stimulate your own thinking.

God invites us into a living relationship. Spirituality is not just a *part* of who we are. It *is* who we are. Spirituality is holistic and all-encompassing. Loving God with all our heart, mind, soul, and strength involves every aspect of our lives.

Spirituality is also a lifelong journey—a journey of faith, a life of walking in the light. It is our privilege to be there with young people during the critical years in which they begin to take responsibility for their own journey, the years that are so crucial to shaping their faith. In the midst of our work with youth, we often find that our work stimulates and enhances our own spiritual growth.

Our personal walk with God is—and will continue to be—the key to our work with youth. Our spiritual growth is our best resource as we seek to invite young people to join us in a living relationship with God in Christ. Without that underlying relationship, everything in this book is just mechanics.

Spirituality cannot be taught academically. It must be experienced, lived. Our function as role models and mentors is to invite. Our joy is to be companions on the journey.

All this requires a great deal of trust on our part. Often we are not there to see how the journey turns out. We see relationships begin, but have no opportunity to see them develop beyond the senior year in high school. We must to trust God. We need a good understanding of the Holy Spirit, one that enables us to trust that God is at work in the lives of the young people we work with and will bring our efforts to fruition.

"Be a good servant . . . nourished on the words of the faith."
FIRST TIMOTHY 4:6b

CHAPTER
1

BIBLE STUDY

"To me the Bible is a very personal thing. It provides spiritual growth and a sense of comfort. It is like a window providing a glimpse into another world and another time. It makes me feel secure knowing that my religion has survived through all the years. I compare myself to those in all the stories and wonder if I have a strong enough faith to deal with the problems they faced."

Courtney
Age 15

"The Bible is all you really have. There's a lot of bad ideas going around and a lot of false teachers. The Bible is from God. It's been tried and it's true. Everything else will go, but God's Word will always remain—and remain the truth."

Ben
Age 16

Many have a mistaken idea of how today's youth react to Bible study. It runs something like the now famous scene from the movie *Ferris Bueller's Day Off*: A boring teacher drones on and on in a monotone voice as the students stare glassy-eyed into nothingness. Some students doodle on paper. Others roll their eyes. One student's head slowly slips down and finally crashes to the desk.

Actually, the opposite is true. As the quotations above indicate, many of today's youth do not have a problem with Bible study. What they have a problem with is how Bible study is done. Bible study does not have to be boring. There are a lot of innovative Bible-study techniques that work well with teenagers. These approaches are interesting and help youth delve into the scriptures in exciting and meaningful ways.

In one church, a small group of students meet in a home after school. They have to hurry to fit in time to study the Bible between school and their evening activities. They spend an hour and a half viewing a videotape, discussing scriptures they have read during the week, exploring how those apply to their lives, and growing closer to one another. They are a part of a Disciple Bible Study group for youth.

In another church, a group of young people are led through an experiential reconciliation exercise as part of an evening youth program. They begin in a circle with arms linked. But as various things that separate people from one another and from God are mentioned, they drop their arms, take several steps back, turn around, and close their eyes. As they stand alone in the darkness, they experience the brokenness and separation of our world. After a few moments, the process is reversed as things are mentioned that unite people to one another and to God. The members of the group take several backward steps toward the center, turn around, and open their eyes to find themselves where they started. As they link arms, a passage of scripture that speaks of God's desire for reconciliation is read. After the exercise, the group discuss things that separate them from others and from God and how God's desire for reconciliation can make a difference.

In a Sunday school class, the students are invited to lie on the floor and close their eyes. The teacher then takes them on a guided meditation on the Nicodemus story in John 3:1-11. With the teacher's help, the students relive the story as if they were there. They place themselves in the story and use their five senses to experience what it was like to be there. Through the meditation, each student becomes a character in the story. What happens in the story happens to them. After the meditation, the class members compare experiences and discuss what they learned from the experience.

The list goes on and on. There are innovative, exciting ways to do Bible study with youth. The purpose of this chapter is to give you the tools you will need for such Bible study. These include understanding why the Bible is so important for spiritual growth, what is age-appropriate for youth, and how we approach the Bible. A set of guidelines is included. But most of the book will be devoted to going over specific Bible-study techniques that work with youth. At the end of the book, you will find a brief bibliography that will point you to additional resources.

Why Is the Bible So Important for Spiritual Growth?

Some people might consider this question unnecessary. All of us know the answer. Or do we? Do we really know what it is that we want to see happen in the lives of young people and how the Bible can play a role in making this happen? In many settings, Christian education goes on with little or no significant contact with scripture. The scripture, if it is brought in at all, is almost an afterthought. In other settings, a great deal of attention is given to memorization and learning the facts or truths of scripture. But even this emphasis may make little or no difference in a young person's life.

What is the real role of the Bible in developing our relationship with God and in growing in our discipleship and commitment to Christ?

What Is the Bible?

The Bible is many things. It's history, poetry, theology, story, biography, and much more. But a few of these things are particularly important for spiritual growth.

The Bible is the church's book. It is our memory as a community of faith. It contains the earliest memories we have of the events that gave rise to our faith. What we know about Jesus, about God, and about what it means to be a Christian is found in the Bible. If we want to be in a relationship with God, the Bible is the place we turn to know more about God. If we wish to be faithful disciples of Jesus Christ, the Bible is the place we turn to learn more about Jesus and what he expected from his disciples.

The Bible contains the word of God. Revelation can come in many ways and through many different means: a sunset, the wind, a worship service, a group of friends, a beautiful piece of music. But for the Christian community, the clearest revelation of God and of God's will for our lives is found in scripture. To attempt to understand God's will for our lives without referring to the Bible and its witness makes no sense in the Christian community.

The Christian community has always insisted that the Bible contains what we need for faith (what we need to know and believe) and about life (what we need to do). The faithful disciple shapes faith and life in dialogue with the scripture.

What Does the Bible Offer?

What does the Bible offer us for spiritual growth? The Bible contains so much that we can sometimes get lost in it. Even a brief passage may contain so many different dimensions that it is difficult to see how it relates to our relationship with God.

Often we get side-tracked by questions and issues that the Bible is not really concerned with. Was the world really made in six days? If so, and the sun wasn't created until the fourth day, how long were the first three days? If Adam and Eve were the only people God created, where did Cain's wife come from?

Dr. W. J. A. Power, an Episcopal priest and seminary professor, has a way of cutting to the core of what the Bible is all about. Dr. Power believes that we can get to the heart of any biblical passage by asking three simple questions:

* What does it say *about* God?
* What does it say *about us* as human beings?
* What does it say *about our relationship with God?*

The Bible is concerned about relationships: our relationship with God and our relationship with one another. When Jesus summarizes the commandments, he reduces hundreds of rules and regulations to two: love God and love your neighbor. In other words, Jesus reduces the complexity of the faith down to its essence: relationship.

Spirituality, at its essence, is relationship—relationship with God and with our neighbor. The Bible, at its essence, is a narrative of the relationship between God and God's people. It also contains what God has to say about relationships. It is concerned with how we grow, develop, and nurture our relationships.

Age-Appropriate Bible Study

Of all the various dimensions of the Christian faith, the one adolescents are most open and receptive to is that of relationship. The teen years key on relationships. Relationships dominate the personal agenda of young people. Teenagers are open to and ready for an understanding of what it means to be in relationship with God, and with one another. It is during the teenage years that the relational agenda that is natural for youth coincides with the relational agenda of the Bible.

Knowing where people are developmentally is helpful in Bible study. Each stage of life has its own issues and concerns, and the Bible speaks to each of these. The key is to know where a group is developmentally and what its issues are. Basing a junior-high study on abstract theological concerns is probably not a productive activity and may give those young people the false impression that the Bible does not have anything to say to them.

Though there are exceptions to any rule, there are trends as to the issues that interest youth:

Junior-high students (7th and 8th grades) are especially concerned with interpersonal relational issues. When allowed to pick the topics they wish to discuss, the topics most often chosen have to do with relationships—with parents, with peers, with God. Sex, sexuality, and relationships between guys and girls are also important. This is the age of identity formation. The key question is "who am I?" When the Bible is used as a resource for dealing with these issues, junior-high students are eager to learn.

Mid-high students (9th and 10th grades) have a different agenda. Their world has begun to broaden and they are concerned about issues in the world. This age, more than any other, is concerned with controversial topics: suicide, homosexuality, the devil, cults, and the occult. Moral and ethical issues move to the center. There is concern about what is right and what is wrong—and why. This group, more than any other, wants to know what the Bible and our faith have to say about these topics.

Senior-highs (grades 11 and 12) are increasingly interested in their place in the larger adult world, with what happens after high school. Key issues include career, separation from parents, living on your own, marriage, personal finances. Depth theological and faith concerns also become important: Is there really a God? How do I know? Is Jesus really *the* way?

These descriptions are generalizations. All the concerns mentioned are present in each group, but certain issues tend to be in the forefront with each. The techniques mentioned in this chapter can be used with all these age groups, but it is helpful to keep these general trends in mind. Having a good technique is only half of the key to success in doing a Bible study with youth. The other half lies in what is called "the teachable moment"—dealing with an issue that is of genuine concern to the group. This means being age-appropriate.

Guidelines for Approaching the Bible with Youth

As you use each of the techniques in the remainder of this chapter, a few simple guidelines will help to keep the Bible study focused in a way that will enhance spiritual growth.

Provide Opportunities, Not Answers

There are times when it is appropriate to provide answers. But most of the time in youth work, what we need to provide are opportunities—opportunities to explore, to encounter, to question and challenge. The adolescent shapes his or her beliefs and life through the process of testing and searching. If we can provide a flexible, safe context in which young people can explore and think through their own faith, we can help them grow in their relationship with God.

If we also can provide opportunities to directly experience God's presence in the midst of life, we can take this process a step further. Many of us remember powerful "camp experiences" when God felt very real and present. One of the challenges in youth ministry is to structure what we do in such a way that teenagers not only have an opportunity to learn about God but also have opportunities to directly experience God. Several of the techniques in this chapter are designed to create such opportunities.

Seize Teachable Moments

There are moments when the young people we work with are more open and receptive than at other times. These are called "teachable moments." Most of the time, the students may not care about a particular truth or point. But then, with little or no warning, a teachable moment will present itself. If a suicide has happened at the local high school that week, the planned Sunday school lesson may be of little or no value. What the class needs, and what the students probably will want to do, is to process their feelings about this loss and try to make sense of it. At an appropriate moment, the class may be very open to something the Bible has to say about life, and death, and God's presence in these, especially if it is shared in a personal, relational way.

Be Open-Ended

Whose agenda do we pursue when we use the Bible with youth? Who decides what is important and what isn't? We know what the Bible says to us, and it's natural to assume that the Bible says the same thing to everyone else. The problem is that it doesn't work that way.

Teenagers are very aware of what teachers—in the public-school system and in the church—want. They know how to play the game of giving the answer that is expected. There is an old joke about a junior-high student who was sitting in Sunday school class and not really paying attention to what was going on. The teacher was trying to find out when a particular event would be happening at the local middle school. The teacher asked the student if he knew. Startled, he responded, "I didn't really hear what you asked, but I know that the answer you want is 'Jesus.'" Adolescents can easily give back the expected answers, and after they go out the door, never have another thought about what was said.

The object of spiritual growth is different. If our object is to develop a relationship with God and our neighbor, and to grow in those relationships, then what we learn needs to shape our lives: our values, our attitudes, our behavior, our decisions, our beliefs.

For this to happen, youth must internalize the content of the scriptures. Its truths must become their truths. We must allow each young person to struggle with the scripture in his or her own way. We can set up the opportunity for encounter, but the encounter itself will be different for each person.

We can't presuppose that our answers will be their answers. They may look at a particular passage (or at the Bible as a whole) differently from the way we do. There has always been a variety of interpretations of scripture within the Christian community. One person takes a passage very literally. Another sees spiritual truths in the passage. Still another sees it as story.

When we work with youth, we can't expect everyone to have the same pat answer. If we believe that the Holy Spirit is at work in each person, then we must allow that the Holy Spirit may work in different people in different ways. When we study the Bible, youth may not see what we see. Our answer may not be their answer. On the other hand, they may see something we have missed. Their answer may teach us something we didn't know about God or about ourselves.

As we work with youth we need to seek to provide opportunities to encounter God, not just teach information about God. Relationship remains primary. The call to discipleship is a call to relationship. A person can know a lot about God without actually knowing God. By trusting the kids we work with, the Bible, and the Holy Spirit, we can free ourselves from the desire to control the process. Instead, we can allow God to use us and the scripture as each individual slowly develops his or her own unique relationship with God.

Utilize Both Sides of the Brain

Modern research has indicated that each side of the human brain performs a different function. The left side is analytical and logical. The right side is intuitive and artistic. Too often, Bible study has been limited to left-brain approaches. The Bible is more than a collection of intellectual propositions to be memorized and adhered to. In addition to left-brain approaches such as memorization and deductive study, we need to incorporate inductive Bible study approaches that are experiential, relational, and intuitive. These right-brain approaches work particularly well with youth. Inductive approaches include the use of motion, art, narrative story, and direct experience.

Be Experiential

One of the insights of contemporary educational theory is that different people learn in different ways. Some are visually oriented, others are more auditory, and still others are more kinesthetic, learning more through movement. Another insight is that different approaches to learning can have a different impact. The most direct and powerful form of learning is experiential. If someone tells us something, we may or may not believe it. And even if we do, it may make little or no difference in our lives. However, when we ourselves experience something, it has a direct and powerful impact on us.

Many of the materials currently available in youth ministry are based on the experiential education model. In experiential education, the goal is to set up a situation in which the class members or individuals can experience something for themselves, or in which they can draw upon their life experiences. But the educational key to experiential learning is to process and debrief the experience afterward, so that the people are aware of what happened and that they gained from the experience.

In one church, a Sunday school teacher decided to prepare a lesson on how we prejudge others. The church had just finished redecorating the youth lounge where the class met. The class members took a lot of pride in the room. The teacher turned furniture over and scattered papers and pencils around as though someone had ransacked the room. The church had been broken into on several occasions, and the teacher was hoping that the class would jump to the conclusion that someone had broken in again.

What the teacher did not know was that another youth group had spent a night in the church during the weekend and had left a note thanking the group for letting them use the lounge. In the process of cleaning up the room the note was discovered, and the class jumped to the conclusion that the visiting group had trashed the youth lounge. The class was outraged and very verbal in its anger toward the visiting group. Later, when the teacher shared what had really happened to the room, the class was able to explore its own tendency to prejudge others.

Use Variety

Anything can get old. This is particularly true when working with teenagers. The word *boring* is the kiss of death. Variety is a key to keeping youth interested. They love to be surprised. They love the unexpected. This is especially true when approaching the Bible. Any Bible study technique, even the most innovative and exciting, can be overused.

Provide Challenging Depth Options

Often, curriculum and classes are set at the lowest common denominator. Many young people are offended if they sense that a class or study is beneath them. If anything, it is better to shoot *above* a class than to shoot *below* them. Youth love to be challenged.

Another implication of this is that we need to provide depth experiences that challenge. Some may not be willing to be involved in an in-depth Bible study. But others will. If we are not sensitive to this need, we run the risk of losing the students who have the most potential in their spiritual growth.

Use Groups and Group Dynamics

Most teenagers love to be in groups. Isolation and being alone are experienced as negative. When doing Bible study with adolescents, we need to be aware of this and use it to our advantage. Group studies and group experiences are ideal. We need to be careful about techniques that involve solitude and depend on the individual's ability to work alone. We can use techniques that incorporate solitude, especially with those in senior high, but techniques that utilize the group will be our mainstay.

"It really means a lot to me to have a chance to study the Bible in depth. It seems like we have covered the same things in Sunday school for years, but never really learn anything new. Last year when we formed a new class to study the Bible in a deep way, I was excited. I like being able to learn new things and be involved in deep discussions."

ERIC, age 18

Use Discussion

The real goal of most Bible-study techniques is to stimulate discussion. Once an experience or activity has been done, the payoff is in the discussion that follows. Discussion is a mutual give and take of ideas, opinions, and experiences, in which young people get a chance to react to the ideas of others and hear how others react to their ideas. A good discussion forces individuals to hear and consider options they would not otherwise have considered.

Discussion is not teacher-based, but student-based. The teacher facilitates or enables a process between class members. The teacher is not the Shell answer person who knows all and tells all. Rather, the teacher helps the class members process their own thoughts and insights. And at appropriate moments, the teacher can enter the discussion as a co-participant.

Allow for Direct Participation

Adolescents have a limited tolerance for sitting and listening to someone else do a presentation. The attention span of a teenager listening to an adult lecture is shorter than the adult would think. In most settings, lecture is not a desirable way to approach Bible study with young people. Techniques that involve teenagers directly through leadership and participation keep the class's interest and enhance the learning experience. Much of the mechanics of the Bible study can be done by members of the class. They can read, write down what is said, lead activities, and lead discussion. In addition, they need to be challenged to encounter the text directly and encouraged to form their own ideas and conclusions.

Know How to Ask the Right Questions

Regardless of the technique used, Bible study is strengthened by knowing the right questions to ask during the debriefing. Three main areas need to be addressed through questions:

(1) *information (what the text actually says)*;
(2) *interpretation (what the text means)*; and
(3) *application (what difference it can make in our lives)*.

Students involved in Bible study need to understand what the passage says, what it means, and how they can apply it to their own lives.

Bible Study Techniques
That Work with Youth

There are literally hundreds of Bible study techniques. Many of these are mentioned in the books listed in the bibliography. Below you will find some techniques that are particularly suited for youth work.

Ignatian-Guided Meditations on Scripture

The basic idea for this form of Bible study goes back to Ignatius of Loyola and has been around for hundreds of years. In an Ignatian meditation, the leader guides the class through a meditation on a passage of scripture and allows the class members to use their imagination to recreate the story and enter into it as participants. Instead of making the passage of scripture an object to be examined and understood, it becomes a reality that the students enter into.

There are four key guidelines for doing an Ignatian meditation:

1. **Place your class within the biblical scene.** It is important for the person to place himself or herself within the story. This is done through the imagination. As the leader guides the class through the story, the listeners are invited to imagine that they are present—in the story.

2. **Have the class members use their five physical senses to make the story come alive.** One teacher I know rereads the text five times, each time inviting the participants to use one of their senses. What would you see? What colors? Where is the light coming from? What would you smell? What textures would you feel?

   A simpler and more direct method is to stop several times at appropriate places during the story and ask the students what they see, hear, smell, feel, or taste.

3. **Invite each class member to become a character in the story.** As the story is read, the listener needs to become a character in the story, not just an outside observer. In some cases, you may want to specify which characters the students are to play. In other cases, you may want to ask them to become characters, but leave the decision as to which character up to them.

19

4. Process the passage as an experience that each class member went through. When the meditation is completed, the follow-up discussion needs to be based on what each person experienced as a participant in the story. What did you see? What emotions did you feel? What happened to you? What did Jesus say to you? How did you respond?

In addition to the four guidelines mentioned above, here are some practical suggestions that will help guided meditations go more smoothly and be more effective:

* Darken the room.
* If possible, have the class members lie on the floor.
* Instruct the students to close their eyes.
* The entire meditation is to be done in silence. Only the leader speaks.
* Soft background music can be helpful.
* Use breathing exercises like those mentioned in the example below to relax the class.

Allow periods of silence after each statement, so that each person can use his or her imagination to experience that part of the text.

EXAMPLE: *Ignatian Meditation Based on John 1:35-42 (Jesus calls his first disciples.)*

Briefly explain to the class what you will be doing. Challenge the participants by telling them that this can be an extremely powerful and moving experience, and that the more they put into the exercise the more they will get out of it.

Have the class spread out across the room and get comfortable. No one should be touching another person or close enough to disturb another. If possible, have the class members lie on the floor. Turn the lights out, and have the students close their eyes. If possible, play soft instrumental music in the background to cover up distracting noises. Ask the students to take several slow, deep breaths, and then slowly read the following meditation. Be sure to allow plenty of time for silence at each space (. . .).

. . . Imagine that you lived a long time ago in the land of Israel . . . You're standing with two friends outside a small town . . . Look around, what do you see . . . feel the sun and the breeze on your skin . . . what sounds do you hear . . . One of your friends is John the Baptist. What does he look like . . . You are standing there because you are waiting to see Jesus of Nazareth. What are you feeling as you wait . . . In the distance, a man is walking toward you . . . John becomes excited, points at him and says, "This is he; this is the Lamb of God." Look at Jesus as he comes toward you . . . What does he look like . . . What thoughts and feelings are you having . . . As Jesus walks by, you begin to follow him. Why . . . Jesus turns around, looks at you, and asks, "What do you want?" . . . After a few moments, you answer, "Teacher, where do you live?" Jesus answers: "Come and see." What is it that Jesus is going to show you . . . You spend the afternoon with him. What do you do . . . What do you talk about . . . Jesus says something to you; it is . . . You reply by saying . . . You ask Jesus a question, something you've always wanted to know . . . His answer is . . . Continue this conversation for a few moments . . . How do you feel about being with him . . . There is something about this man . . . You realize that in him you have found something you have been looking for. What is it . . .

Have the class members open their eyes and form a circle. Debrief the experience by asking the following questions. Seek to get several responses to each question.

1. What was that like for you?
2. How does this differ from the way we normally study the Bible?
3. How difficult was it to get into the story?
4. What did you see or hear?
5. What did Jesus look like?
6. What was your reaction to John the Baptist?
7. How did you feel when Jesus first came up?
8. When Jesus asked you what you wanted, what did you answer?
9. What did you talk about with Jesus?
10. What feelings did you experience in his presence?

After the debriefing, have someone read John 1:29-34. Ask the class how the Ignatian meditation changed the way they see that story.

This type of Bible study is particularly useful with stories or narratives. You can use the meditation above as a model and do this approach with any of hundreds of stories in the Bible. In the Old Testament, you might want to use stories of youth or others who have encounters with God: the call of Samuel, the call of Jeremiah, Elijah's encounter with God at the mountain. In the New Testament, the Gospel stories and the book of Acts are particularly helpful.

Theological Bible Study

The basic idea behind this approach is to read the text and ask the three questions that Dr. Power says are central to any text:

* What does it say about God?
* What does it say about us as human beings?
* What does it say about the relationship between the two?

For this approach, it will be important to divide the class into three groups, each of which will read the passage and answer one of the questions. Then have the three groups report on what they discovered. It is important that the class not get sidetracked into other issues, such as "Did it really happen?" or "How could it have happened?" The group is reading only for theological content: God, us, relationship.

Is it also important that the teacher not be the answer giver, but only one of many searchers. The source of information is the text itself, not the teacher.

EXAMPLE: *Genesis 1:1–2:3 (the first story of creation)*

Begin by having someone read the story to the whole class. Explain the process you will be going through, and then divide the class into three groups. Assign each group one of the three topics. Give the groups several minutes to re-read the passage and answer the questions. Make sure each group has a facilitator who will keep things going, a recorder who will keep notes, and a reporter who will make a verbal presentation.

Have each of the groups make its report. Possible answers might include:

God	Us	Relationship
powerful, creator, source of everything, brings order out of disorder, creates good	creature, a part of creation, made in image of God, have responsibility for all of creation, good	we are dependent upon God, God put a lot of effort into creating us

As each group finishes its report, see if anyone else in the room can add anything on that topic. Repeat this process with the other two groups. When you are finished, ask:

* What have we learned about God from this passage?
* How does this fit what you already knew about God?
* What surprised you?

Repeat these three questions on the other two topics.

Dialogue and Encounter

In this approach, several individuals or small groups work independently on a passage and then discuss what it means. The key to this approach is to push for alternative viewpoints, rather than consensus. The power of this approach lies in the likelihood that a collection of people, working independently, are more likely to encounter the richness of a text.

EXAMPLE: *Isaiah 44:9-20 (warning against idol worship)*

This passage is one that can be taken in a lot of different ways. At a literal level, it is humorous. Yet it quickly invites the reader to consider the idols we make for ourselves. By dividing a class into groups or giving several individuals the assignment of reading the passage on their own, you ensure a variety of opinions and observations. Allow time for each individual or group to read the passage. Have them be prepared to speak about the three major dimensions of meaning:

(1) *information (what it says)*;
(2) *interpretation (what it means)*; and
(3) *application (what it means for us)*.

Expect a lively give and take at the third level.

Paraphrase and Reverse Paraphrase

Paraphrase and reverse paraphrase are both delightful ways to make a text come alive. Both require students to use their own creativity. In paraphrase, the student or class rephrases the text in different language. Most often, the students are simply invited to put the text in their own words. However, this can be a lot more fun if it is done from a particular slant. Your kids know of groups in their schools or in society that have their own idiom or forms of expression. A text can be paraphrased from one of these perspectives: valley girl ("like totally cool"); Mr. T; Bart Simpson; church lady; televangelist; old West; southern drawl—the possibilities are endless. Current TV shows or movies provide many possibilities. If several different groups or individuals paraphrase the same text in a variety of ways, the results can be hilarious, and also insightful.

Reverse paraphrase is paraphrasing—but with a twist. In reverse paraphrase, the wording is reversed so that the meaning is exactly the opposite. This has a shock effect that forces the person to think about what the words really mean, as in this reverse paraphrase of a portion of Psalm 23:

> The Lord is not my shepherd,
>   I have nothing,
>   I get no rest,
> God tosses me about in a raging river,
>   My spirit is battered,
>   God guides me into evil,
> Even when I walk in the midst of life
>   I am terrified,
>   for God is against me.
>   I fear everything
> For I have been abandoned by God . . . .

Both these approaches work well with passages that are so familiar they have lost their effect. But they also work well with passages that are difficult to understand. It is important to debrief the experience by asking the class what new insights they gained from the exercise.

Role Play

Role plays are another form of Bible study that work particularly well with stories, especially stories that have characters or issues that teenagers can identify with. In a role play, students take on the roles of characters and then act out the scenario in the passage. There are two main ways to do this. One way is to stick with the passage as though it were a script, and simply have the class act out the scene as written. One twist on this approach is to have the actors place the story in a contemporary context.

Another way is to have the class members assume the roles of the characters in the story and then have them go beyond what the text says and continue the story in a way they feel is faithful to the characters.

EXAMPLE: *Genesis 37 (Joseph and his brothers)*

A role play of this passage would include several main characters: Joseph, Israel (his father), a couple of brothers (or sisters), and his brother Reuben. Have the class study the story and the characters in the story. Make sure that any questions are answered. Then have volunteers take the roles of the characters and role play the story.

Afterward, ask each person what it was like to be the character he or she portrayed. What did this person think? Feel? Why did this person behave the way he or she did? End by asking the class members what they learned about the story by doing the role play.

Another option is to interview the characters from the role-play and have them answer questions "in character," as they feel their characters would answer the questions.

Gestalt Role Play

In a gestalt role play, one person plays two roles, or two or more persons can play the two parts, or the two sides of one person. The roles are symbolized by chairs. When a person is in one chair, he or she is one character. When the person moves to the other chair, the other character is present and speaking.

EXAMPLES:

This can be done in several ways. One way is to involve two separate characters. For example, in Matthew 4:1-16 (the temptations of Jesus) one chair could represent Jesus, the other chair, Satan. The person doing the role play acts out the drama of the temptations by switching back and forth between the two chairs and the two characters. Afterward, the class could even interview the two characters as to why each said or did certain things.

Another approach is to let the two chairs represent two parts of the same person. In the case of Paul's inner struggle in Romans 7:14-25, one chair could represent the side of Paul that wants to be good, while the other chair represents the side of Paul that wants to be bad. Many teenagers would readily identify with a conversation between these two sides of Paul.

At a more complicated level, you could have several chairs, representing the various parts of the body described in I Corinthians 12:12-30. It would be easy to have a lively discussion between the various parts (hand, foot, eye, ear). For a twist, this could be followed by a discussion in which the parts are renamed to fit a more contemporary and specific situation: youth group, older adults, parents, the church staff, *or* nerds, jocks, socials, skaters, etc.

When the discussion is over, the various "characters" could be interviewed as to why they said or did certain things. This could lead into a discussion of issues that are relevant to the group—that is, why certain people feel unimportant or others seem to have an inflated sense of self, and what Paul's statements have to say about that situation.

Devotional Reading

The key to this approach is to read the Bible from the perspective of asking what it is that God has to say to *me* right *now* through *this passage*. Devotional reading assumes that the text is not just a historical document, but that—through the Holy Spirit—God can and does still speak through the scripture. In this approach, the reader seeks not so much to understand as to hear and obey.

In using this approach, it is helpful to give each individual time to read the text privately and reflect on it. Afterward, bring the group together and have them discuss what they feel God is saying to each of them.

EXAMPLE: *I Timothy 4:12 (Young people are important to God.)*

Don, an 11th grader, is active in church and mature beyond his years. He has a lot to offer. Yet often, he does not feel that he is taken seriously by adults. His ideas and contributions are disregarded simply because he is not an adult.

When Don read this passage, the first thing that stood out for him was "Let no one disregard you because you are young." As Paul speaks this word of encouragement to Timothy, he speaks it to Don and to countless others. Don also remembered what Jesus said to his disciples concerning children: "Forbid them not, for to such is the kingdom of God." What Don hears is that he is important to God, that God takes him seriously, even if others do not.

But as Don reads on, he gets a clearer idea of what he can actually do when he is not being taken seriously: "Be an example to all the believers in the way you speak and behave, and in your love, your faith, and your purity." When Don read these words at summer camp, he heard God speaking to him, saying something he needed to hear. He was important in the eyes of God, and he wasn't the first person not taken seriously because he was young. He also gained an insight into how he can be taken seriously: He can be an example, through his life, of what a Christian is called to be.

Meditating on Scripture

Meditating on scripture is similar to devotional reading, but it is freer. In meditation a person will read a passage and then reread it, looking for things that "jump out." It may be a word, or a phrase, or an image. It may be a thought provoked by what the text says. In meditation this becomes the starting point. The person meditating on scripture then begins to free-associate, or think about the word, phrase, or image, to see where it may lead. The meditator is not limited by what the scripture is saying. The scripture becomes a starting point.

EXAMPLE:

A junior-high student may read a passage about honoring your father and mother, and the meditation may lead this person into thinking about his or her relationship with a particular parent, the problems in that relationship, and what needs to be done to make the relationship more healthy.

Journaling

Both devotional reading and meditation on scripture can be done without journaling, but journaling enhances both. A journal is like a diary. The person writes down his or her thoughts, ideas, feelings, questions, and so on, for further reflection. In Bible study, journaling becomes a means of gathering one's thoughts and feelings so that they can be expressed later. Journaling exercises can include letters to God (what you want to say to God), or letters from God (what you think God might say to you), or dialogues with God. It may be as simple as a few words or sentences, or as complex as entries that go on for pages.

EXAMPLE:

In a Bible study, the group would first read the passage, then spend time journaling thoughts and feelings. Afterward, it would be important for the group to come back together and share what they have written. The more trust there is in a group, the more depth there can be to this exercise. Journaling works best in a weekend retreat setting or in an ongoing small group in which the members are committed to one another.

Biblical Debate

In a biblical debate, two opposite sides of an issue are debated, using the scripture as a basis. The book *Controversial Topics for Youth Groups* (Edward N. McNulty [Group Publishing, 1988]) uses this approach. No matter what the topic is—abortion, homosexuality, war—the approach is the same. Each side in the debate attempts to be faithful to the scripture, to see how what it has to say sheds light on the topic.

EXAMPLE: *Abortion*

These debates usually follow a semi-formal format. Divide the class into two groups and assign their positions. One will be pro-choice, the other will be pro-life. Give both sides scripture references that could be used by their side. Tell them that their assignment will be to argue *from a Christian perspective,* using the biblical passages you have given them (and any others they can think of) as resources. Give the two groups time to do research and to prepare their arguments.

Next, have each side present its argument. Give both sides the same amount of time. Then give both sides a few minutes to prepare their rebuttals. Each side then has a few minutes to argue against what the opposing team has presented. After this is done, tell the class that in a Bible study, it is not important to have one side win and one side lose. Instead, after the debate, move the class into a discussion of what they learned about the topic.

One interesting twist on this approach is to find out which side of an issue the members of the class agree with and have them take the opposite view. Those who were pro-life would take the pro-choice position and vice versa. This forces the class members to consider the other side of a position. This does not mean they must agree with it. But it will help them understand it better.

Spectrum Bible Study

The idea behind spectrum Bible study is to get as many different interpretations of a passage as possible, and then see what all of them—collectively—tell us about the passage. But rather than the interpretations being each person's private opinion of what the text says, as in dialogue and encounter, the class looks at the passage from a variety of pre-determined positions. Spectrum Bible study uses four of these approaches: *literal, allegorical, spiritually true, only a story.*

"I remember the time we were studying abortion in our evening youth group. We decided to research the topic and have a debate. We split up into two groups; one group for abortion and the other against it. Then the sponsors made all those who were against abortion research the pro-choice position from a Christian viewpoint, and then argue for it. The pro-choice group did the same with the pro-life view. It really made me think about the issue in new ways. It didn't change my beliefs, but it made me realize that it is more complicated than I had thought."

JANA, age 13

EXAMPLE:

For spectrum Bible study, divide the class into four groups and assign each group one of the four approaches. The literal group would read the passage from the perspective of taking every single word at its literal meaning. The allegorical group would assume that everything in the text means something else. (An example of this approach is found in the Gospel of Matthew. In Matthew 13:4-9, Jesus tells the parable of the sower. A few verses later, in Matthew 13:18-23, the parable is explained as an allegory. Everything is really something else. All the types of seed and soil become types of people.) The spiritually true group would look for the religious truth in the passage—what it says about God and the things of God. The story group would look at the passage only as a story.

Each group reports its findings based on its own approach. Then the whole class discusses the following four questions:

* What is each point of view actually saying?
* What value does each position attempt to uphold?
* What are some problems with each view?
* What are some implications of each view?

Finally, the class is asked what it learned about the passage through this approach.

Exploring Personal Problems Through Bible Study

People have always used the scriptures to deal with personal problems and issues. As a particular form of Bible study, this approach begins with a personal issue and then moves to the scriptures as a resource. The group will begin by focusing on a common problem, issue, or experience, and then bring selected passages of scripture to bear on the issue to see what light they shed.

The procedure has three steps: (1) a sharing time of dealing with the personal problem; (2) a time devoted to looking at selected scriptures (a topical Bible that has scripture referenced to key topics can be a valuable tool); and (3) a period of discussion in which there is dialogue between the problem and the scriptures.

This approach lends itself naturally to adolescents and is the model behind a lot of contemporary curriculum.

EXAMPLE: *Romans 7:14-25 (Paul's inner struggle)*

Begin by involving the class in a discussion of times when they have not understood their own behavior. Model what you are asking for by telling of a time when you either did something you knew was wrong or did not do something you knew was right. Have several others share their experiences.

Ask: Why do we do this? Involve the class in a discussion that focuses on what it is like to want to do one thing—and do another. Then have someone read Romans 7:14-25 and see whether the class members can identify with Paul's feelings. You might want to supplement this passage with some stories from the scriptures which illustrate this human tendency—for instance, the story of David and Bathsheba in Second Samuel, or Jesus in the Garden of Gethsemane (Matt. 26).

Have a member of the class read verse 24 out loud. Ask: What is Paul talking about? How does God make a difference when we think we can't do the right thing? Finish the Bible study by focusing on how God's love and forgiveness can make a difference when we feel as if we can't pull it off.

Relational Bible Study

This approach to Bible study is similar to the theological one, in that it focuses on particular aspects of a Bible text. In this approach, however, the focus is on relationships. The text is read for what it has to say about relationships. There are four levels of relationship to be focused on:

1. Our relationship *with God.*
2. Our relationship *with ourselves.*
3. Our relationship *with other people.*
4. Our relationship *to the world.*

The key to relational Bible study is not to get side-tracked into data or detail, but to remain focused on the relational nature of the Bible. There are a lot of things we may not understand at a rational level. There is a lot we won't understand due to the changes in culture and worldview over the centuries. But the basic qualities of relationships remain unchanged over the ages. Human beings still struggle with the same relational issues they did three thousand years ago: love, passion, greed, lust, alienation, jealousy, anger, joy. In the stories of the Bible, we see ourselves and our relationships.

EXAMPLE: *Psalm 8*

Read the psalm out loud. Answer any questions anyone has about the psalm. Then divide the class into four study groups. Assign each group one of the four dimensions of relationship. Tell the groups that all four are in the psalm, but some will be easier to spot than others. Give the groups time to read the passage and identify the aspects of relationship they are looking for.

Bring the groups back together and have each group report its findings. After each report is given, involve the class in a discussion of what the passage is saying and what it has to say to us today. End by asking: How does looking at the relationships in this passage help us understand the passage? How does it help us understand ourselves better?

Affective Bible Study

Often in Bible study, we focus on the cognitive content of the passage. For some texts that may be adequate, but for many it will be inadequate. The Bible is a story of people and relationships. It brims with emotion. To ignore the emotional or affective content of the Bible is to drain it of much of its power.

Affective Bible study focuses on the emotional content of a passage to discover what the feelings expressed can say to us. This approach is especially appropriate for the psalms or for narrative stories. But it can be used in almost any text, including a highly theological text like the one in the example below. Affective Bible study has four steps:

1. The passage is read with attention to the emotions present or expressed.
2. Two questions are asked to help the class deal with the emotional content:
   * What feelings are present?
   * Why do you think the author or the character in the story feels this way?
3. There is a time of personal sharing, facilitated by two questions that connect the passage to the life of the group.
   * Have you ever felt this way? When? Where? (Encourage the students to narrate a story from their own lives that parallels the one in the passage.)
   * Is anyone experiencing this right now?
4. Through two questions, seek guidance from the passage in dealing with the personal issues expressed:
   * Did the writer or character in the story experience any resolution with the issue presented there?
   * Is there anything we can learn from the Bible passage that can help us with our issue?

EXAMPLE: *Galatians 3:1-5*

Have the group begin by reading the passage. Use the first two questions to help the group identify the feelings present and why Paul feels so strongly. Since this is a theological passage and the portion being studied is part of a larger section (chapters 3–4), you may want to read the longer passage and be prepared to give a brief explanation of what is behind Paul's anger—something like, "Paul has discovered that some of the people in the church at

Galatia who had accepted Jesus and become Christians have now abandoned everything they have been taught and have returned to their earlier religion."

The key here is not to focus on what happened there in Galatia two thousand years ago. Rather, you want to use the issue and Paul's anger to evoke similar experiences or feelings within the class.

Once you feel the class has a basic understanding of the text, move to the third step. Have the class members identify times when they have felt angry or betrayed by others. Invite the members to tell their own stories in a time of sharing.

Reserve some time to move to the fourth and final step. Can the class see anything in the way Paul dealt with his anger that would be helpful to them? If the students can't find anything in the passage as read, invite them to read on for several more verses.

Transformational (Behavioral) Bible Study

Unlike many of the other Bible study techniques in this chapter, transformational Bible study focuses on how the Bible can motivate and enable behavioral change. It takes the biblical mandate to "be transformed into the image of the invisible God" seriously. In theological terms, transformational Bible study sees the scripture as a resource for the ongoing process of Christian formation—growth in holiness. Transformational Bible study uses four key questions:

* What truth does this passage teach? (What should we believe?)
* How does the passage reveal and rebuke error? (What should we reject?)
* What can be learned from this passage to help correct faults and put things right? (How can we change?)
* What instructions does this passage give to direct our daily living? (How should we behave?)

EXAMPLE: *II Timothy 3:14-17*

This passage is ideal as an introduction to transformational Bible study, since it argues for the transformational nature of scripture itself. Have the class read the passage and then give everyone a few moments to make notes and write down any questions that come to mind. Ask the first question above and invite the group members to give their responses. Encourage discussion and interaction between class members. Repeat the process with the other three questions.

End by asking: What do we need to do this week to put this passage into practice? Allow plenty of time for this step, as it is the heart of transformational Bible study. Encourage each person present to struggle with the question and form his or her own individual response. End by having all of them share what it is they need to do. End with a prayer in which you ask for God's strength and guidance.

Dialogue with Current Events, Music, or Media

This approach seeks to take something from contemporary life to raise an issue, and then bring the scripture into a dialogue with that item. It is helpful if something from contemporary life has captured the attention of the group, whether it is a news item, a song, or something from a movie or TV.

EXAMPLES

In the case of current events, the newspaper, news magazines, or television news can be used as a resource. If the local newspaper reports a change in policy by the school board on locker searches at the high school, there will be a high level of interest in this topic. This article could be used as a springboard to explore the right to privacy versus the right to safety for the school and its students. A variety of passages could be used for this purpose.

A popular song on the radio, or one the group listens to, could be used to raise a faith or moral issue. A few years ago, the rock group Depeche Mode had a song called "Policy of Truth." The song begins with a recording of Richard Nixon's voice, saying, "I want to tell my side of the story," then goes on to reflect on the nature of truth and lying. The relevance of this topic for the Christian community is obvious. But by starting with the song, a group might be more motivated to discuss the topic.

Other media also provide opportunities to find material: movie releases, television shows, articles from magazines. Many of these raise and deal with important faith issues and issues of concern to youth. The basic format for this approach would be the same, no matter what the resource.

* Use the resource to raise the issue. Hand out the newspaper article, play the song, etc.
* Have the group discuss the resource and see what issues it raises for them.
* Have the class read one or more passages of scripture that deal with that issue or are relevant to the issue.
* Have the class carry on a dialogue between the issue raised and the scripture resource.
* Have the group summarize how the scripture might help in dealing with the issue.

Depth and Encounter

This study method combines several of the methods mentioned above for a more powerful effect. It combines paraphrase, depth Bible study, and transformational Bible study.

EXAMPLE: *Galatians 5:13-26*

Begin by having the class read and paraphrase a portion of this passage, verse by verse. You may want to select a portion of the text for the whole class, or divide the passage into smaller parts and assign it to different groups or individuals.

Next, ask the class to consider what would happen if this passage and what it is saying were taken seriously. How would their lives change? Divide the class into small groups of about five and have them share their answers to this question.

Finally, reassemble the total group and have volunteers share what was discussed in each group. Ask: What challenges or impresses you most deeply from this passage, or from the discussion?

Movement

At the beginning of this chapter were several examples of exciting, innovative ways to study the Bible. One of these uses movement. That one was written by Joani Schultz and is found in *The Giving Book*. But the same principle can be used for countless passages. The idea is to use movement to express or encounter what the text is talking about. Breaking physical contact, walking away, turning around, closing eyes—all symbolize and act out the brokenness of our world. Walking back toward the group, turning back toward the group, reestablishing physical contact, and opening eyes—each of these symbolizes reconciliation. "Trust" exercises, in which people are passed around physically or caught when they drop, become a way of physically acting out faith. Printed curriculum resources are filled with activities like these, and once you have done a few of them, it becomes easy to create your own.

Disciple *Bible Study for Youth*

This chapter has been devoted to Bible study techniques, not to prepackaged Bible study programs, of which there are many: Bethel, Trinity, Kerygma, and so on. *Disciple* is listed here for two reasons: (1) because it is a uniquely powerful approach to Bible study that focuses not just on academic knowledge, but on responding to God's call to discipleship. It also utilizes many of the techniques and ideas advocated in this chapter—small groups, experiential learning, discussion, and so on. And, (2) the Youth Edition of *Disciple: Becoming Disciples Through Bible Study* is specifically designed to be used by youth.

Disciple is a systematic survey of the Bible that lasts for nine months. It is not exhaustive, in the sense that every verse in the Bible is read. Rather, it is comprehensive, in the sense that major portions of most books are read and the basic themes of the Bible are covered.

In the *Disciple* program, a small group of young people (around 12) covenant with the group leader to spend nine months together, reading the Bible from the perspective of spiritual growth. The key question behind the whole package is "How can I become a more faithful disciple?"

Disciple has two key elements: daily home readings of scriptures, and a two-hour weekly group session. Each student has a study manual that gives assignments and additional resources. The students read and make notes for six days and rest on the seventh. The readings also include questions that are personal rather than academic, and a section on "The Marks of Discipleship," in which each person is invited to respond to the call of discipleship in a personal way.

The group sessions begin with a brief time of personal concerns and prayers. Then a brief 10-minute video segment is shown. One of the unique qualities of *Disciple* is that each week, through the videotape, the class has access to an outstanding biblical scholar and teacher. The tape is then discussed, and the group moves into a day by day discussion of the scripture readings and participants' comments and questions. Next, the class will experientially do a Bible study. The "teacher helps" section suggests a variety of approaches, including several of those in this chapter. The group session then ends with personal sharing, based on "The Marks of Discipleship."

It is worth noting that *Disciple* is different from many other forms of youth Bible study, in that the adult leading the group is not a teacher in the traditional sense. Rather, the adult functions as a group facilitator. The information does not flow from the teacher to the group.

It flows from the Bible to the group members and from the group members to one another. One of the key reasons for the required training of *Disciple* teachers is to help them understand that they are not to "teach" in the traditional way.

Disciple has two major drawbacks. The first is financial. With the study manuals, videotapes, and required training, it is expensive. The cost is in the hundreds of dollars. The second drawback is in the area of commitment. *Disciple* involves a major commitment of time and effort on the part of those who take it. It is not for everyone.

Counterbalancing these two drawbacks is my personal conviction that *Disciple: Becoming Disciples Through Bible Study*, Youth Edition, is the single most powerful tool currently available for serious study of the scriptures with youth. It works. It does things nothing else can.

For more information about *Disciple* Bible study, call toll free 800-251-8591 or 800-672-1789, or write to *Disciple*, P.O. Box 801, 201 Eighth Ave. South, Nashville TN 37202-0801.

"For everyone who asks receives."
LUKE 11:10

2

PRAYER: SPEAKING TO GOD

Kelly was leading the prayer time during our regular evening youth fellowship. As members of the youth group shared joys, concerns, and prayer requests, Kelly led the group in the response, "Hear our prayer, O Lord." Then she shared one of the most eloquent prayers I have ever heard. The prayer was from her heart and spoke directly to the concerns that had been expressed. The whole room was moved.

As Kelly prayed, my mind flashed back to an evening two years before, the first time I had asked her to pray in front of the group. Her answer had been immediate and emphatic: "I can't pray!"

I then asked, "Can you say, 'Dear God, thank you for everything. Amen'?" She gave me a funny look and answered, "Sure, I can do *that!*" So I asked her to do it. And she did. Afterward, she looked up at me with a smile and beamed with a look of accomplishment.

Kelly's problem wasn't that she couldn't pray. She could and she did. Her problem was that two things stood in the way of her praying. The first was her understanding of prayer. She associated prayer with what she had seen ministers and other adults do. Her models were long, elaborate prayers that seem to go on and on and mention everything under the sun. Kelly was convinced that she couldn't do that. She was not aware that a prayer could be short and simple.

The second problem Kelly faced in praying was that no one had ever taught her how to pray. Others had always prayed for her. She never had the opportunity to practice and develop this skill. For prayer is a skill. It is learned. And whatever can be learned can be taught.

Jesus Teaches His Disciples How to Pray

There is an interesting story in the eleventh chapter of Luke, in which the disciples of Jesus ask him to teach them how to pray. We are familiar with this passage because it contains the Lord's Prayer, but the situation itself is worth looking at:

[Jesus] was praying in a certain place, and after he had finished, one of his disciples said to him, "Lord, teach us to pray, as John taught his disciples." He said to them, "When you pray, say:

> Father, hallowed be your name.
> Your kingdom come.
> Give us each day our daily bread.
> And forgive us our sins,
>   for we ourselves forgive everyone indebted to us.
> And do not put us to the time of trial."

Luke 11:1-4

For those of us who work with young people and want to help them develop a personal spiritual life, there are several interesting things about this passage. First, what provoked the request to be taught was that Jesus himself was praying, and the disciples observed him doing this. Jesus modeled prayer in his own life. And this modeling had an effect on the disciples. They wanted to learn how to do what Jesus was doing.

Second, the disciples acknowledged that they did not know how to pray. Prayer was not a skill they were born with, but one they needed to develop. Like Kelly, they needed to be taught.

The third thing that stands out is the Lord's Prayer itself, which Jesus gives as a model. In stark contrast with much of the prayer we have in the church, Jesus' prayer is a model of simplicity. With few words, it speaks directly to the key issues of life. In the version of the Lord's Prayer found in the Gospel of Matthew, Jesus specifically warns the disciples against praying in ways that are pretentious:

> When you are praying, do not heap up empty phrases as the Gentiles do; for they think that they will be heard because of their many words. Do not be like them, for your Father knows what you need before you ask him.

Matthew 6:7-8

Prayer is a skill. It is learned. This means that it can be taught. We only need to remove unnecessary obstacles to prayer and give the youth we work with opportunities to develop this key skill. This and the following chapter will help you think through your own understanding of prayer, give you some guidelines for working with youth, and give you numerous techniques that you can use with your group.

What Is Prayer?

One of the obstacles we need to remove is the common confusion about what prayer is and is not. Almost anything can and has been said in the name of God in prayer. Abuses of prayer abound, both outside and within the church. It's little wonder that many young people are either confused about prayer or turned off by it. Recently I listened as two of our junior-high students were parodying a popular televangelist praying. What they had accurately picked up on was a grotesquely distorted understanding of prayer. They were quite good. They had the fake intonation down pat. They knew how to say "Jes-us" with just the right effect. And they knew how to make outlandish requests of God. But did they know how to pray?

Several centuries ago, the Protestant Reformer Martin Luther made a couple of interesting observations about prayer that are still helpful today. Both of his observations are in the form of what prayer is *not*.

First, prayer is not telling God something that God otherwise would not know. When we pray we are not bringing God up to date on what is going on. As Jesus commented to his disciples, our Father knows even before we speak. Prayer does not tell God anything.

Second, prayer is not a means of forcing God to do something that God otherwise would not do. Prayer is not leverage on God or a way to manipulate God. What God does, God does because of who God is, because of God's gracious nature. Prayer does not make God do anything.

If prayer is not telling God something God otherwise would not know or talking God into doing something God otherwise would not do, then what is prayer? It's clear that if Martin Luther is correct, then we have eliminated much of what usually passes for prayer.

Martin Luther's point is that prayer is not for God at all. Prayer is for us. We don't pray because of the effect it has on God. We pray because of the effect it has on us. Prayer is a tool God has given us for our own benefit. Prayer does not change God. It changes us and helps us.

The Christian faith is profoundly relational. Spiritual growth has to do with developing our relationship with God. Prayer is conversation. It is talking to God and listening to God. Prayer makes us aware of who we are, of who God is, of what we need, and from whom we get what we need. Through prayer—in all of its many forms—we enter into communion and conversation with God.

Historically, the Christian faith has emphasized two major forms of prayer: *active prayer* (talking to God) and *passive or dispositional prayer* (listening to God). Like Bible study, prayer is at the center of our faith. We grow in faith as we develop our relationship with God. Common sense dictates that a relationship—any relationship—requires communication. Not only that, but it requires regular, ongoing communication. Any relationship can drift and deteriorate if it is not continually nurtured.

Relationships also require two-way communication. We need to learn how to speak to God, but we also need to learn how to listen to God. This chapter will focus on techniques for active prayer, or talking to God. The next chapter will cover techniques for dispositional prayer, or how to listen to God.

Guidelines for Teaching Youth to Pray

As was the case with Bible study, prayer is more than just mechanics. Because it is profoundly relational, what you are trying to teach is not so much mechanics as how to nurture and develop a relationship. In using any of the techniques below, there are a few simple guidelines that will help.

Model Prayer

It is still true that young people learn more by what they see us do than by what they hear us say. One of the most effective tools we have in teaching adolescents how to pray is our own ability to pray. Our ability to model not only how to pray but our ability to model the importance of prayer in our own relationship with God is crucial for youth. Jesus' disciples saw that prayer was important to Jesus because they saw him praying. Our youth can learn the same thing from us.

Practice Prayer

The best way to learn how to pray is to pray. Studying prayer or talking about prayer can take us only so far. Like the familiar NIKE commercial, there comes a point when we "just do it." Not only do we need to be praying, but we also need to make sure that the kids are praying. The more they pray, the more meaningful prayer will be to them and the more prayer will become integrated into their lives.

Provide Opportunities to Pray

If the teens we work with are to practice prayer, then we need to find opportunities for them to pray. Every meeting can open and close with prayer. We can pray over concerns. We can use every opportunity we can to lift feelings, concerns, issues, to God in prayer.

Require Prayer

I am personally convinced that prayer should not be an option. When we gather, we pray. When we depart, we pray. When we worship, we pray. When we have pains and sorrows, we pray. When we have joys, we pray. The practice of prayer comes first. An appreciation for prayer will follow. It is a mistake to ask a group if they *want* to pray.

We need a lot of things in life that we may not want at a particular moment. Prayer is too important to be left to a vote or to our fickle feelings. John Wesley once made the comment that we should "preach faith until we have it, and then when we have it, preach faith." In much the same way, we should pray until we develop an appreciation for prayer. Then, when we have an appreciation for it, we should pray.

Call on Kids to Pray

There is no easy way to pray the first time. There is a certain amount of awkwardness and discomfort to learning how to pray. Several years ago I was shocked by the practice of another youth minister who would routinely call on a youth to pray without warning. He would simply say, "Jim, pray for us." And Jim would. Jim was uncomfortable. Jim stumbled over his thoughts and his words. But he prayed. And, like Kelly, through this stumbling, awkward process, Jim learned how to pray. There is nothing wrong with calling on kids to pray. They may be uncomfortable. But the act of praying itself is the only way to overcome that discomfort.

Use Techniques That Involve Everyone

Many of the techniques below allow a number of people to be involved in a prayer, rather than focusing in on one person. Prayer forms, such as circle prayer, which involve everyone in the group make it easier for those who are uncomfortable with prayer.

"Every year, when the new 7th graders come into our youth group, I get so mad because they do not have an attitude of prayer. Being able to voice my prayer concerns in youth worship, hear the prayer request of others, and take time at the altar to pray are important to me. I really miss it if I don't get a chance to pray each week."

STACEY, *age 14*

Use Silence

Sometimes it is helpful to ask for a volunteer, rather than designating a particular person to pray. When you do this, allow plenty of time for silence. Most adolescents are more uncomfortable with silence than they are with prayer. If you ask for a volunteer and then allow for an extended period of silence, someone will usually volunteer in order to end the silence.

Teach "an Attitude of Prayer"

Several years ago I worked with a volunteer who taught me to appreciate what she called "an attitude of prayer." What she meant by this was a tone or a mood. She taught our group that when we were in an attitude of prayer, there was to be a definite shift from what we had been doing. An attitude of prayer included becoming quiet, focusing on what we were doing, and using a tone of reverence. When someone said, "Let us pray," there was a perceptible change in the room. She taught me that kids can easily learn this and come to highly value it. Once an attitude of prayer has been taught, the kids themselves become the ones who enforce it.

Communicate Expectations

I have often heard the complaint that teenagers, especially those in junior high, are incapable of taking prayer or worship seriously. They won't sit still. They talk during the prayer. They won't focus on what is going on. My own experience is exactly the opposite. I think one of the issues here is a failure to communicate expectations. As a general rule of thumb, the more I expect, the more they come through. When I have problems, it is usually because I have failed to communicate what is expected.

Young people don't know what is expected until we tell them. They don't know what to do or to avoid, until we clearly communicate our expectations. And teenagers need to be continually reminded. We cannot tell them what is expected and then expect that to do the job. We need to repeat ourselves again and again.

Deal with Disruptions

A lot of disruptions can be avoided by taking preventative measures. When we clearly communicate expectations, teach an attitude of prayer, and use our relationships with the youth, many potential disruptions never arise. But kids are kids. They will make mistakes. They won't think.

When disruptions arise, three guidelines are helpful. First, confront the issues directly and immediately. It will rarely get better if it is ignored. Be honest. Tell the group what is bothering you. Don't use names or point out any particular person. Share your concern about the disruption to the group as a whole.

Second, use the group. Ask the group how it feels about what is going on. In many instances, the group is just as bothered—if not more so—than you are about the disruption.

Third, after the event, if you have to, speak to the individual who was disruptive. Never do this in front of others. This makes you the heavy and that youth the hero to his or her peers. Deal with it one on one. Tell the young person what bothers you, what you want, and then ask him or her to help you.

Allow Them to Determine the Content of Their Own Prayers

Several years ago, one of the volunteers on our team came to me, upset by a prayer that was shared by a junior-high girl in worship. The group had been in a time of prayer. Those present were invited to lift their concerns to God. Several of the group had shared significant concerns: divorce, death, illness, broken relationships. Then one seventh-grade girl prayed for her dog that had just died. The volunteer felt that this was inappropriate, that it destroyed the serious mood of the prayer time because a couple of senior-highs had laughed.

As it turned out, this was the girl's first experience of death, and the dog had been in the family as long as she had. The dog was more than a pet. It was a lifelong friend whom she had lost and for whom she grieved. It was this very deep and sincere pain that she had lifted to God in the prayer. We need to be extremely careful when we label something appropriate or inappropriate.

Provide an Environment of Prayer

Prayer works best when it is like the air we breathe. Prayer should not be sporadic, occasional, or alien. It should always be there, woven into the fabric of all we do. It should be a natural part of every activity. The more we weave prayer into our various activities and events, the more natural prayer will seem to the young people we work with.

Allow Time for Prayer to Develop

Prayer is a spiritual discipline. It is a skill. Skills and disciplines are not learned overnight. First we learn to crawl. Then we learn to toddle, then walk, then run. Developing the prayer life of individual youth or of a group takes time and patience. We can't rush the process. We can only facilitate it and nurture it. And ultimately, we must trust the young people we work with and trust that God is at work in their lives.

Active Prayer Techniques That Work with Youth

Most of the time the praying we do involves what is called active prayer, or speaking to God. Active prayer involves addressing God with our concerns, our needs, our agendas. In active prayer, we do the speaking. Listed below you will find 24 ways you can use active prayer with youth groups.

Sandwich Prayer

A sandwich prayer is simply prayer that is used in opening and closing an activity. It makes the statement that what we are doing is done in God's name and in God's presence. Anyone can do the praying, and it can have any content. Prayer becomes the bracket around the activity.

Circle Prayer

In a circle prayer, the group forms a circle, and each person around the circle, in turn, adds to the prayer. You can use any one of several techniques listed below: word, sentence completion, and so on. You may want to give individuals the option of passing. One way you can do this is to have the person who wants to pass squeeze the hand of the next person. The prayer then skips on to the next person. There is also an advantage to requiring each person to pray. The key is to strike a balance between gentle and loving pressure to pray (and thereby grow), and permission to pass.

Word Prayers

Word prayers are prayers that are limited to a word or short phrase. In this form of prayer, each person thanks God for something, or asks God for something, but is limited to a word or phrase. The leader sets up and models the form, then each teen adds a word. The leader might say that we all thank God for one thing. Then the responses might include: parents, friends, this group, and so on. This is less intimidating for young people who are afraid of prayer.

Sentence Prayers

Sentence prayers are extended word prayers. In these prayers, teens are limited to one sentence (usually short!). This can be done in a circle-prayer format, or responsively, as in Prayers or Concerns.

Open-ended Prayers

These are sometimes called sentence completion prayers, a special form of sentence prayers in which the leader sets up the topic and the group members fill in the blank. Examples include: "Lord, I thank you for . . . "; "Lord, help me with . . . "; "God, I'm sorry that . . . ."

Build a Prayer

In this special form of circle prayer, one person begins the prayer and leaves it open-ended, as in "God, today we thank you for . . . ." The next person in the circle will pick up where the last person left off and continue, but also leave it open-ended. This continues around the circle until the last person adds a part and ends with "Amen." This can become frivolous. But it also can be a powerful and effective form of prayer as each personal literally builds on the prayer of the person before. A prayer might look like this: Dear God, I pray that we . . . uh, might be thankful for all you have given us, such as . . . our friends, our parents, and . . . .

Responsive Prayer

This is sometimes called a "say with me prayer." It's like a responsive reading, except that group members will repeat whatever the leader says. Any prayer can be done this way. If we were to do the Lord's Prayer as a Say with Me Prayer, it would look like this: Our Father (Our Father), Who art in heaven (Who art in heaven), and so on.

Popcorn Prayers

In a popcorn prayer, various members of the group, wherever they are, stand up one at a time to give a prayer, then sit down. There is no pattern to this. It is like kernels of popcorn that randomly pop up, then go back down. The content of the prayer can vary. Group members can share concerns, joys, or whatever. In one form of this prayer, short statements can be written on sheets of paper and then distributed to group members to be read. The act of standing allows one person to be the focus of the prayer at that moment, gives the group a point to focus on, and helps the speaker be heard.

Quaker Prayers

This form of prayer takes its name from the Quaker tradition of "waiting on the Lord." In this prayer form, the group enters into a time of silent prayer. Before the prayer begins, group members are invited to share prayers "as the Spirit leads." During the time of silence, group members may lift up prayers as they feel led. Sometimes no one prays. At other times a few people will pray. Occasionally, a large number will pray. The prayer ends after a prolonged silence indicates that all who wish to contribute to the prayer have done so. The key to this form of prayer is not to be afraid of extended silence at the beginning of the prayer.

Written Prayers

Group members can read prayers that are written down. They can get these from books, or they can write them out themselves. Written prayers are most effective when they are short—anything much beyond 15 to 30 seconds can get boring. Written prayers are especially effective with those who are afraid of praying. Having the prayer written down and in their hands helps them deal with their anxiety.

Songs

Many songs have lyrics that are prayers. These can be read like written prayers. Or they can be sung. The Wesleyan Grace and Doxology are examples that many of us use. Group members could use songs from the hymnal, songs from contemporary songbooks, or songs from contemporary Christian artists.

Silent Prayers

Silence allows group members to express their concerns in ways that they might not do verbally. They can be more honest and open. Allowing a time of silence, with no expectation that anyone must say anything out loud, can be an effective prayer tool. In this way, people are able to say their own prayers in a way that is appropriate to them.

Altar Prayer Time

Many adolescents like altar prayer time. It gives them a chance to spend time in silent prayer in a structured way. The physical movement to and from the altar is also important. Soft background music and subdued lighting are ways of enhancing the mood or atmosphere. It is important not to rush altar prayer time. Most teens will pray for a minute or two, but occasionally someone will need a longer time.

ACTS Prayers

ACTS is an acronym for four traditional ways of praying: *adoration, confession, thanksgiving,* and *supplication.* These refer to the *content* of the prayer—what it is we're talking to God about.

Adoration refers to praising God for who God is, as in "Dear God, you are a good God because . . . ." This form of prayer enables group members to practice praying without focusing on themselves. It also allows them to focus on who God is and why God is special.

Confession refers to being open and honest before God about our own shortcomings, as in "Dear God, I am sorry I . . . ." Confession is important because all of us carry hidden wounds, hurts, and guilt that need to be forgiven. It allows youth to seek forgiveness.

Thanksgiving refers to thanking God for what God has done in our lives, as in "Lord, I thank you for . . . ." This is probably the most common form of prayer for youth and the easiest for them to get into, but it still needs to be practiced. Prayers of thanksgiving allow us to be thankful and to be mindful of the fact that much of what we have comes from outside ourselves. It keeps us from being consumed by self.

Supplication refers to asking God for help, as in "Lord, help me to . . . ." This prayer has a dual focus: our need and the source of help. Prayers of supplication teach humility.

Eightfold Prayer

The eightfold prayer is the same as the ACTS prayer, except that the content of prayer is divided into eight topics rather than four. *Adoration, confession,* and *thanksgiving* remain on the list. Supplication is divided into *petition* and *intercession.* And three more forms of prayer are added: *aspiration, commitment,* and *acceptance.*

Petition refers to supplication for ourselves, as in "God, help me to . . . ."

Intercession refers to supplication for others, as in "God, help Tim to . . . ."
Though similar, these two forms of supplication allow us to make a distinction between our needs and the needs of others. Both are appropriate, but are distinctly different.

Aspiration refers to praying that we might become more like what God would have us to be, as in "Lord, help me to be more loving when . . . ." Aspiration is important because it allows us to focus on the ultimate goal of discipleship—to become more Christlike.

Commitment refers to dedicating ourselves to new attitudes and behaviors that go beyond what we have been in the past, as in "Lord, I commit myself to . . . ." Prayers of commitment allow us to focus on the heart of the Christian faith—our commitment to God and to God's kingdom, and our commitment to walk with God in our daily lives.

Acceptance refers to opening ourselves to receive what God would give us, as in "Jesus, I accept your forgiveness," or "Thy will be done." This is probably the hardest form of prayer. It is difficult for most adults, yet it is not beyond the reach of youth.

Prayers and Concerns

This technique enables group members to voice their experiences—both their ups and their downs, their joys and their concerns, their positive and negative experiences—in a prayer time. This can be done in worship or in another setting. One variation is to have the group respond with a short phrase after each prayer, so that the whole group participates in the prayer. Possible responses include "Lord, hear our prayer" or "This is our prayer, O Lord."

These responses are important for several reasons. At one level, they enable the group to participate in and affirm each prayer or concern. At another level, the response clearly indicates when one prayer has ended and the group is ready to hear another. This is especially important in large groups, when an individual's prayer may not be heard by everyone. In these settings, the leader can repeat the prayer or concern so that everyone can hear it, then lead the group in the response.

Praying for Concerns

In this format, members of the group will lift up their concerns. As each concern is lifted up, another member of the group will agree to pray for that concern. This prayer can be voiced immediately after each concern, or it can be done in the closing prayer. If the closing prayer is a circle prayer, the people who agreed to pray for specific concerns do so as the prayer comes to them. In another form, the closing prayer begins in silence, or with the statement, "Let us pray . . . ," and then each person is free to add to the prayer, including those who have agreed to pray for specific concerns.

Journaling

Journaling involves writing a diary to God. The person writes openly about his or her thoughts and feelings, as in a diary, except that God becomes the one to whom the diary is written.

Or the diary could be turned into a spiritual-growth journal. In this case, the content would be limited to things that affect the person's spiritual journey or relationship with God.

Letters to God

This is a variation of the prayer journal, in which members write a letter to God, much as they would write a letter to anyone else. They write about the things they want to address—their concerns, hopes, struggles, and so on.

"I never will forget the first time I journaled. It wasn't really hard. It was like writing in a diary, except you wrote to God. It helped me to see God like a person that I can talk and express myself to. I had never really thought about that before. Since the retreat where I learned this, I find that I occasionally still need to talk to God in this way. I don't do it all the time. But when I am really struggling with something, it helps."

CARLA, age 15

Dialogue Prayers

This is a modification of the letter to God, in which group members begin a conversation with God by writing a question or statement, and then continue with what they think God would say in response. There is usually a strong correlation between what God says in these dialogue prayers and how God is presented in the scriptures.

If there is a concern that any individual may come up with some wildly distorted understandings of God, this fear can be dealt with by having members read their dialogues within small groups. The groups can correct any such wild statements. The pattern continues as a dialogue or conversation with God (or Jesus) is carried on.

Prayer Partners

In this technique, two people agree to pray together. Each will hear the concerns of the other, and then each will pray for those concerns. This can be done holding hands. Each person may pray for his or her own concerns or for the other person's. This can be done silently or out loud.

Intensive-Care Units

The ICUs are small groups in which the members agree to be involved in a few minutes of intimate sharing and prayer. Some youth groups form ICUs during the opening or closing few minutes of their meeting time. In these small groups, the members share openly and honestly about how they are doing and then pray for one another. In an ICU, it is important to take time to hear the concerns before praying. The prayers should be in response to the concerns and mention the specific concerns.

Prayer and Share Groups

A prayer and share group is like an ICU, except that it lasts longer and is more in depth. A prayer and share group might meet for an hour or more. During that time, members share things that are important to them, and the group would try to be loving and supportive. As a person finishes sharing, the group briefly prays for that person in light of what was shared.

This type of group can take a variety of forms. Some groups let anyone join who wants to participate, since there is no set theme or agenda. Other groups are keyed to special needs and issues, such as divorce, death, life transitions (e.g., graduation), parent/youth communication, and so forth. See *Sharing Groups in Youth Ministry* (Abingdon Press, 1991), for the guidelines and resources needed to organize and lead a prayer and share group.

Blessings and Bandages   yes? no?

In this exercise, one person chooses another member to hold his or her head. The person then lies down on the floor, face up, with his or her head in the other member's lap, and eyes closed. The others in the group place their hands on the person and then pray for that person. The person on the floor is not allowed to say anything until the exercise is over. This is an extremely powerful exercise and is especially effective with people who feel they are not important or that others do not care for them.

"Everyone then who hears these words of mine . . ."
MATTHEW 7:24

PRAYER: LISTENING TO GOD

As a freshman in high school, Erika went off for her first "quiet time" as part of a spiritual-life retreat. She was skeptical about how she going to use thirty minutes by herself. She also was very aware that following the solitude time, there would be ninety minutes of free time, and she was looking forward to being with her friends. Thirty minutes sounded like a long time to be by herself, but she was willing to give it a try.

Two hours later, an excited Erika couldn't wait to share the results of her time alone. She had spent the entire two hours by herself under a tree, reading a passage of scripture, thinking about it, and writing a letter from God. She confessed that "it took the first thirty minutes just to get calm and put other things out of my mind. It was only then that I could really get into the exercise. Then, the time flew." Through the letter from God, in which she expressed what she thought God *might* say to her, based on the scripture she had read, Erika was able to work on a key issue in her life—one that had been bothering her for some time. For her, the letter was "an answered prayer." Years later, she still treasured the letter and its place in her spiritual-life journey.

Tim was ecstatic: "That was cool! Can we do that again?" The *that* to which Tim referred was a guided-imagery meditation, in which he and several other junior-high students had been invited to use their imagination to meet and have a conversation with Jesus on a seashore. The leader walked the group slowly through the meditation, allowing plenty of time for them to use their imagination and fill in the blanks.

Both these stories illustrate a whole dimension of spirituality often overlooked in our work with young people—listening to God.

The Loss of "Listening to God"

All too often, the spiritual disciplines we have been taught focus on *talking* to God rather than *listening* to God. It is easy to slip into a spirituality that focuses on what we do, rather than on what God does.

The irony is that throughout the history of the Christian faith, there have been well-developed forms of prayer and Bible study that allow us to listen to what God is saying to us. But many in the church, including the youth, have little contact with these prayer forms.

Historically, the church has affirmed two basic forms of prayer: *active prayer*, in which we talk to God, and *passive* (or *dispositional*) *prayer*, in which we listen to God. Active prayer, which we examined in chapter 2, includes most of the prayer forms we normally use: petition, intercession, thanksgiving, praise, confession, adoration. What all these have in common is that they are ways we can express ourselves to God. Even when we are invited to a time of silent prayer, this usually is devoted to active prayer, spoken mentally rather than out loud.

Within our history there was another prayer form, one that was devoted to learning how to "dispose" ourselves to listening to God. Recent physiological research and "left brain/right brain" theory reinforce this second approach. We now know that the two halves of the brain function in different ways. One side (the left) is analytical, logical, and rational. The other side is intuitive and imaginative. The spirituality that most of us are familiar with is left-brain spirituality—analytical and rational. We "study" the Bible. We address ourselves to God in active prayer. In a sense, we think out loud to God.

What is missing for many of us is right-brain spirituality—using our imagination and our intuition, as well as silence, to let God speak to us. Historically, many of the ancient saints of the church used these right-brain prayer forms. Perhaps the best known was Ignatius of Loyola, the founder of the Jesuit order. Ignatius developed many of the tools we will be using.

This chapter is devoted to exploring how youth can be taught to *listen* to God. The injunction of the psalmist is "be still and know that I am God." It has never been easy to put aside the cares and distractions that surround us, and in the modern world, it is becoming increasingly difficult. Yet young people have a natural affinity for these prayer forms—and enjoy them immensely.

Dispositional Prayer: Key Definitions

Dispositional prayer is the opposite of active prayer. Rather than providing a way to address or speak to God, dispositional prayer provides ways we can listen to God. It uses time-tested techniques that allow us to "dispose" ourselves to be open to God. We can't make God speak to us. But we can dispose ourselves to listen and attend to God's presence in our lives. There are two main forms of dispositional prayer: meditation and contemplation.

Although these two forms of dispositional prayer are often confused, they are actually the opposite of each other. *Meditation* is a technique in which we are invited to focus on something and then see what happens. We might meditate on a passage of scripture. In that case, we would read the scripture and then see what comes to mind. The idea is that God might speak through the free association that goes on in meditation. Meditation also can focus on a word, an image, or a variety of other objects.

Contemplation is the opposite of meditation. Instead of focusing on an object, the idea is to try to empty the mind of all content. Historically, this is called kenosis, or *emptying*. In contemplation, a person tries to go totally blank, and then let God speak into the silence.

Components of Dispositional Prayer

In working with youth, there are six key components to using dispositional prayer. These six allow us to relax and dispose ourselves to be open to the actual prayer techniques.

Silence

To listen to God, a person must first be quiet. Speaking and all other activity need to cease. As long as we are talking, we are not listening. The first requirement for listening to God is a closed mouth. For many youth this will be a new experience. Fortunately, silence is a learned skill. With time and experience, most youth can develop a real appreciation for a quiet time.

Mental quietness is also important—and much more difficult to achieve. The techniques below are designed to occupy the mind so that it too can be silent. But ceasing to talk out loud is the beginning point.

"Many times my prayers can become so overcome with requests, and hopes of God that I forget to listen for an answer. That's not to say that I hear God's voice in my head or anything. But if I am focused and my mind is free and clear sometimes the answer will just come to me. I guess it's sort of like meditation only I call it prayer. If I can just clear everything out of my head and just "talk" to God, then the connection that is formed can often lead me to an answer. Many times when I choose not to listen to God, it's because I don't want to hear the answer. Many times I try too hard to work through things on my own and "take control" of my own life, but in the process I lose the understanding that I need God in my life and if I will only open my heart and my mind I will hear him."

MICHELLE, *age 16*

A Place Apart

The Gospels report that Jesus often went away from the crowds to "a place apart" to pray. Distractions are still a major barrier to listening to God. In order to listen to God we need to find our own place apart, one that is free from distractions and interruptions.

In our world, this is increasingly difficult. In our day-to-day lives we are rarely alone. For many of the youth we work with, this is further complicated by the presence of personal electronics that enable us to bring the world with us even when we are alone. To be "apart," we not only must be removed from the distractions of others around us; we also need to be free from the distractions we may bring with us.

When doing dispositional exercises, it is helpful to have young people remove themselves from any distractions. Sometimes this literally will mean each person going off alone to an isolated place. In other situations, it may mean simply spreading out over a room so that they are not touching one another and are as removed—as possible—from the distracting presence of others.

Breathing/Relaxing

Even when we have removed the distractions around us, we may still be preoccupied by the distractions within ourselves. Like Erika, we find that once we are alone, we are unable to relax. We may feel the tensions of the day or find our mind preoccupied with some of the things we have tried to leave behind.

For thousands of years people have used breathing exercises (breath work) and relaxation techniques to help center and release the cares we bring with us. This takes a variety of forms. One of the simplest techniques is to breathe slowly and deeply from the diaphragm. This will increase the level of oxygen in the blood and make it less likely that an individual will fall asleep during meditation. It also has a calming and relaxing effect on the mind.

Another technique is to lie down and mentally go through the body, tightening and releasing various sets of muscles. You might start with the feet and then slowly move up to the head. As you come to each set of muscles, tighten, hold the muscles tight for about three seconds, and then release. Do this slowly and take about five to ten minutes to relax. Individuals can do this on their own, or a group leader can take the group through the relaxation exercise.

Other people like to "breathe scripture." You can do this by taking a simple verse, such as "Be still and know that I am God," and mentally repeating it over and over as you slowly breathe deeply in and out:

Be still (slow breath in)
and know (out)
that I (in)
am God (out).

Whatever technique is used, the point is that these breathing and relaxing exercises are not meditations in themselves. They are merely a way of relaxing and centering, so that the person will be ready for the meditation.

Music

When we are quiet, we become aware of the distractions around us. There is traffic in the street. The stomach of the person next to us is making noises. In a group setting, we become aware of the noises others make around us. Soft, mellow music can be used to mask these distracting sounds. It functions much like "white noise." Any soft, relaxing music will do, but it is best if it does not have a definite rhythm and is not familiar. Rhythms and familiar pieces of music draw the listener's attention away from the meditation and into the music itself.

The best music is the kind that can be played in the background and not noticed. A lot of music in the New Age section of the local music store can be used in this way. Some people object to anything with a "new age" label. But while new age philosophies and religious practices are often antithetical to Christian beliefs, much of the music in this section is not tied to the philosophy, but is merely a contemporary form of soft music. Originally, this type of music was labeled "anti-frantic."

Some Christian artists, such as John Michael Talbot, have composed music specifically for Christian meditation. Much of the music under the labels Narada, Private Music, and Windom Hill is very helpful. You can create a desired mood for a meditation by selecting music to go with the meditation. Some youth leaders have made sound tracks for meditations by linking several pieces of music together.

Using the Imagination

One of the key elements for dispositional prayer is the use of the imagination. In dispositional prayer individuals are invited to use their imagination to enter into a passage of scripture, a story, or an image. The imagination becomes the vehicle by which the person can cut off the outside world and explore the inner world.

During the meditation techniques below, it is important that the person be allowed to use the imagination. The instructions should be minimal and suggestive. When leading a meditation for others, we need to set it up so that the persons use their imagination. And we should avoid anything that hampers the imagination.

Adequate Time

Dispositional prayer takes time. For Erika, it took thirty minutes just to get to the point where she could do the exercise. If she had given up after twenty minutes or so, she never would have had the experience she had. Dispositional prayer cannot be rushed or controlled. The idea is to dispose ourselves by using the elements discussed in this section, so that the techniques mentioned below can have a chance to work. Adequate time, without rushing, is crucial.

Techniques for Dispositional Prayer

Ignatian-Guided Experiences of Scriptures

One of the most powerful tools for dispositional prayer is an Ignatian-guided meditation on scripture. Although specifically designed to help make the scriptures come to life, the elements developed by Ignatius centuries ago lend themselves readily to other techniques. In its Bible study form, the technique is a way of enabling the individual to move beyond simply reading the biblical story. It enables the person to enter into the story as a full participant, so that what happened in the story happens to the person doing the meditation. In an Ignatian meditation there are four keys:

53

1. Use your five senses to experience what was happening in the story. What would you have seen? Heard? Tasted? Felt? Smelled? Focus on the story and the scene. Use each sense to make the story come alive. What colors do you see? What sounds? Can you feel the wind? The sun? What conversations could you have heard? The list is endless.

2. Use your imagination to enter the story and become a part of the scene. Imagine yourself in the story. You were there. Go through the story as a participant. Become a part of the story. Don't read the narrative as a detached, objective outsider. Read it as one who was intimately involved with what was going on.

3. Identify with the story emotionally. What would you have felt if you had been there? How would what is happening affect you? What are your reactions? What specific emotions does the story evoke?

4. Become one of the characters in the story. Choose a character, or just let yourself naturally gravitate to one of the characters. Experience the story from the perspective of the person in the story. Or better yet, experience the story from more than one character's perspective. Experiencing the story from the perspective of each of the characters gives a richness to the story that we otherwise miss.

There are two ways to approach an Ignatian meditation. The first way is to go through a passage of scripture several times. First the person reads the passage one time for each of the five senses. Each time, the person focuses on a different sense to experience the story from that perspective. Then the story is read a sixth time, and the reader places herself or himself within the story. Then the story is read one final time, and the reader becomes one (or more than one) character in the story.

The second approach may be more helpful in youth ministry. In this approach a leader takes a group through the meditation. The participants lie on the floor as the leader takes them through the breathing exercises and the meditation. In this form, the various dimensions of the meditation are done simultaneously by the leader. The people are invited to enter into the story, and the leader provides the hints that help them become involved. The following meditations can give an idea of how this is done.

EXAMPLE: *John 1:35-39 (Jesus calls his first disciples.)*

Relax . . . take a series of slow deep breaths . . . in . . . out . . . in . . . out . . . imagine that you are living 2,000 thousand years ago in the land of Israel . . . you live near Jerusalem . . . you have heard of this new prophet called Jesus . . . but you have never met him . . . it's late in the afternoon . . . you're standing with two other people . . . look around for a moment at the scene . . . what can you see . . . feel the wind . . . the warmth of the sun . . . listen to the sounds around you . . . smell the air . . . what are you feeling as you stand there? . . . in the distance you see someone walking toward you . . . the person looks unfamiliar . . . but there seems to be something special about this person . . . what do you sense about this person? . . . one of the two persons you have been standing with is John the Baptist . . . what does he look like . . . what is it like being there with him . . . why are you there . . .

John now points to the man walking toward you and says, "Look, there is the Lamb of God" . . . what does John mean by this . . . what do you feel . . . as Jesus walks by, you and John and the other person who was with you begin to follow Jesus . . . why are you following him . . . Jesus now turns around and looks at you . . . what does he look like . . . what expression do you see on his face . . . what are you feeling as Jesus looks at you . . . what are you thinking . . . Jesus then says to you, "What do you want?" . . . answer him . . . you ask him where he lives . . . Jesus then says, "Come and see" . . . why did you want to know where Jesus was living . . . why does Jesus want you to go with him . . . what is it you will "see" if you follow . . . you begin to follow Jesus to where he is going . . . what do you see as you journey with him . . . who else is around . . . and how are they reacting to him . . . how are you reacting . . . you come to the house where Jesus is staying . . . take a few moments to look at the house . . . and the people Jesus is staying with . . . you spend the rest of the day at the home with Jesus . . . what do you do . . . what do you talk about . . . (allow a few minutes for a conversation to take place) . . . bring your awareness back into this room . . . to this time and place . . . what stands out from the meditation you just went through . . . what is it that you want from Jesus . . . what is it that you find when Jesus invites you to "come and see" . . . what did you talk about with Jesus . . .

EXAMPLE: *John 3:1-8 (Nicodemus comes to Jesus at night.)*

You are in the city of Jerusalem at the time Jesus was alive . . . you're walking down a street late at night . . . you are alone . . . you have heard about this new prophet, Jesus from Galilee . . . he is in your town . . . what thoughts and feelings does his being here stir up . . . you are a religious leader . . . you have been raised in your faith . . . you know the Bible, and others respect you . . . you are going to meet Jesus . . . you are going at night because you don't want your friends to know you are going to see him . . . why are you going to meet Jesus . . . what is it you want . . . why are you going alone, at night . . . what is it you are afraid of . . . you're walking down a dark street . . . what do you see . . . what do you hear . . . what is the temperature like . . . can you smell anything . . . what emotions are going through you . . . ahead, in a courtyard, are a group of people . . . they are gathered around a fire, talking . . . one of them has his back to you . . . somehow you sense that this is the person you are looking for . . . what goes through your mind as you get close to him . . . he turns to look at you and smiles . . . what does he look like . . . he doesn't say anything . . . how do you feel . . . what will you say . . . you find yourself giving Jesus a compliment . . . how much you have heard about him . . . how he must be a great teacher to be able to do the things he does . . . how he must be from God . . . now Jesus speaks . . . he speaks directly to you . . . but his comment doesn't seem to fit anything . . . he doesn't seem to acknowledge your compliment . . . instead, he says something strange . . . he says, "Unless you are born again you cannot see the kingdom of God" . . . take a few moments for these words to sink in . . . what does he mean . . . and why is he saying this to you . . . you find yourself confused . . . you fumble for words, and mumble something about it is impossible for someone your age to be physically born a second time . . . Jesus now speaks a second time . . . he seems to sense your confusion . . . he adds, "Unless you are born through water and the Spirit, you cannot enter the kingdom of God. Don't be surprised when I say that you must be born from above.

Remember, the Spirit of God blows wherever it pleases; you hear it, but you can't tell where it is coming from or where it is going. That is how it is with all who are born of the Spirit" . . . for a few moments, engage Jesus in a conversation about what he means . . . find out why he is saying these things to you . . . why does he keep saying, "You cannot enter the kingdom of God unless" . . .

Guided Imagery Meditations

In a guided imagery meditation, Ignatian techniques are used, but the meditation is no longer just an exploration of a biblical story or scene. Guided imagery meditations take the scripture text as a point of departure, and then expand on an element in the story. The following meditation is based on Jesus' parable found in Matthew 13:45-46: "Again, the kingdom of heaven is like a merchant looking for fine pearls; when he finds one of great value, he goes and sells everything he owns and buys it."

The idea of a valuable pearl representing God's gift of the kingdom becomes a point of departure. In the meditation, the listeners are invited to imagine encountering Jesus on a seashore and having Jesus give them a "pearl of great price." The listeners provide the content to the pearl. The leader merely sets the story up so that the listeners have a chance to use their imagination to explore what it is that God is giving.

EXAMPLE: *Matthew 13:45-46 (the pearl of great price)*

Imagine that you are walking along a seashore . . . it's late at night . . . take a few moments just to enjoy the scene . . . look out over the ocean . . . listen to the sound of the crashing waves . . . feel the waves as the surf comes over your feet . . . feel the cool evening breeze . . . you are walking down by the seashore because something is troubling you . . . something is not right in your life or is missing . . . what is it that brings you to the seashore alone late at night . . . in the distance you see a figure walking toward you . . . as the figure comes closer, you sense that this is no ordinary person . . . there is something special about this person . . . something tells you that somehow, for some reason, Jesus is walking town the beach toward you . . . what does he look like . . . why is he here . . . why is he walking toward you . . . what do you feel . . . as he approaches, you stop at the edge of the surf . . . without saying anything, Jesus walks over beside you and looks into your eyes . . . he seems to know you . . . he senses what is going on inside you . . . he knows your struggle, your pain, what is missing in your life . . . Jesus smiles . . . he reaches down into the surf and pulls out a strange looking shell . . . it looks like a clam . . . Jesus opens the shell and holds it up for you to look at . . . inside it is something that looks like a large pearl . . . but it is unlike any pearl you have ever seen . . . look closely at it . . . look into it . . . it is clear . . . looking into it is almost like looking into a window . . . you sense that if you look into it carefully, you will be able to see . . . something . . . you look up at Jesus . . . into his eyes . . . you sense care and warmth . . . you sense that Jesus has a gift for you . . . if you will look deeply into the strange pearl, you will see the gift that God has to give you . . . you look at the pearl . . . Jesus places the strange pearl in your hand . . . you gaze deeply into it . . . you see . . . take a few moments to really look at what is in the pearl . . . what is it that you see . . . why is this important to you . . . what is God's gift to you . . . what is Jesus offering you . . . look back at Jesus . . . take a few moments to share with him what his gift means to you . . . look back into the pearl . . . you look up and Jesus is gone . . . you are standing alone on the beach . . . but the pearl is still in your hand . . . God's gift to you is still there . . . end with a brief prayer in which you thank God for the gift you have received.

Guided Fantasies

A guided fantasy uses Ignatian techniques but is totally devoid of any contact with scripture. Here the leader sets up a fantasy in which the person gets to meet God, or Jesus, or have some lived experience that invites the person into reflecting on his or her relationship with God. This idea is as old as Plato's famous cave scene in *The Republic*, where God is encountered.

The following fantasy was suggested by the science fiction movie *Brainstorm*, in which a person has an afterlife experience and is brought back. This fantasy takes the medical technology suggested in the movie and uses it as a vehicle for an afterlife experience in which the person has a direct experience of God.

EXAMPLE: *A Life-After-Death Experience* Life after Death Phenomenon are questionable in their christian association and are embraced by the New Age movement

It's late at night and you are being taken to a secret military installation . . . a short time ago, a group of people came to your house and said that they needed your help with a secret experiment . . . and now you are at the installation . . . you walk inside . . . what are you feeling . . . what do you see . . . you enter a strange room . . . the walls are lined with strange electronic equipment . . . in the middle of the room is a platform for someone to lie on . . . a man in a white coat thanks you for coming . . . he repeats what he said earlier . . . they are doing experiments on life-after-death experiences . . . the equipment can suspend all life functions—heart, breathing—so that a person can technically "die," then be brought back to life . . . they want your help . . . because you are a Christian . . . they said that the last person who went through this experiment claimed to have met God . . . they want you to go through the experiment, and then share what you experience after you die . . . you hear yourself agree . . . you are on the platform . . . they are giving you a shot . . . you find yourself drifting off . . . then, nothing . . . you have the sensation of floating . . . you can't see anything . . . or feel anything . . . in the distance you see a dim light . . . you find yourself moving toward the light . . . you begin to feel excited as you draw closer . . . there is something special about this light . . . as you come closer, other lights begin to appear and fly around you . . . you hear something that sounds like music . . . in the center of all the lights and music is the light you first saw . . . you are getting very close . . . you feel a warm, tingling sensation all over . . . you sense that you are floating in the presence of God . . . inside your head there is a voice . . . it is the voice of God . . . God speaks to you and says . . . you feel . . . feel God's love like the warmth of the sun . . . feel God's care like a wind that blows across your body . . . share with God how you are feeling . . . you feel yourself now being drawn back . . . somehow you know the experiment is over, you have to return . . . what is it you will take with you from these few moments . . . what will you say when you are back in the room . . .

EXAMPLE: *Meeting God in a Cave*
(This fantasy develops Plato's idea of meeting God in a cave.)

You're walking through a forest . . . up above, you can see the sun breaking through the leaves . . . beams of light strike the ground around you . . . you feel the coolness of a breeze . . . you hear the sound of a small stream nearby . . . a small animal runs past you . . . a bird flies overhead and cries out . . . up ahead you can see a cave . . . you walk over to it . . . you look inside . . . you feel a cool breeze coming out of the cave . . . you put your hand on the side of the cave to guide you as you walk in . . . you walk farther and farther . . . it is very dark . . . and quiet . . . as your eyes slowly adjust, you see some kind of light in the distance . . . you slowly begin to walk toward the light . . . the cave turns to the right . . . the light seems to be coming from around the turn . . . you go around the corner and see . . . you are in a large chamber of the cave . . . in the center of the chamber is something unlike anything you have ever seen before . . . it is a light . . . a flame . . . or something . . . it is hovering in the air . . . it is moving around . . . you suddenly become aware that the room is pleasantly warm . . . you feel a tingling on your skin . . . a chill goes up your spine . . . there is something about this light . . . it's almost alive . . . then—somehow—you sense that you are in the presence of God . . . somehow God is present with you . . . in this room . . . in this flame . . . you feel . . . what thoughts are going through your mind . . . suddenly a voice seems to be inside your head . . . it speaks to you and says . . . you say . . . the voice invites you to ask any questions you have . . . you think for a moment then ask . . . suddenly the light begins to grow . . . to fill the room . . . you can feel the gentle warmth of the light all over your body . . . the light seems to go right through you . . . you feel . . . loved . . . complete . . . and now it is time to go . . . you start to leave . . . you turn back one last time and say . . . then you slowly leave the cave . . . you are aware that you have changed . . . the experience in the cave has had an effect on you . . . it is . . . you are different because . . .

Conversations with God/Jesus

This idea was suggested and developed in the book *No Instant Grapes in God's Vineyard* by Louise Spiker. The basic idea is the same as the Ignatian exercises above, except that the person writes down his or her thoughts, feelings, and experiences on a sheet of paper. Begin with a question or statement to God (or Jesus) and then write down what you think God (Jesus) might say in response. Then respond to God's (or Jesus') comment. Continue in the form of a conversation between yourself and what you honestly think God would say to your questions and statements.

One approach is to read a passage of scripture first, then let the scripture set the tone and boundaries of the conversation. In this instance, you would write down what you think God would say *in light of how God is depicted in that scripture.*

Another approach is not to limit God's comment to a passage of scripture, but honestly write down what you think God might say, based on everything you know about God.

58

EXAMPLE: *A Conversation with Jesus*

Me: Jesus, I've been struggling with what I am going to do with my life.

Jesus: Tell me about the struggle.

Me: There are so many things I could do. But I'm not sure which I really want to do or which is best.

Jesus: I have given you talents and abilities. What do these tell you?

Me: Well, I'm good with people. I enjoy them. I seem to get along well with people, and they seem to like me.

Jesus: How could you use this ability?

Me: In lots of different ways. But I would also like to make a good living. I would like to be able to afford all the good things of life.

Jesus: Have I taught you anything that would help you with this?

Me: Well, I know that money isn't everything.

Jesus: Can it make you happy?

Me: It's important. But I know it isn't everything.

Jesus: How does that help you make a decision about your future?

Me: I know that I shouldn't decide just based on how much I will earn.

Jesus: What will you base your decision on?

Me: On what I know I can do well. And on what makes me happy.

Jesus: What about others? Should you think about other people and the world around you when you make this kind of a decision?

Me: I'm not sure.

Jesus: Will your decision affect others?

Me: I guess so. I know that I could do something that would help others and make the world a better place.

Jesus: That's a thought.

Me: It is. It's an important thought.

"Listening to God for me has always been one of my biggest challenges. I tend to try so hard to do everything on my own, that it takes some big event for me to turn to God for help. But more recently, I have started to understand that there are a lot more times in my life when God is trying to talk to me, and I'm just not there to listen. We go through life with varying awareness levels of God, and often it is only when we need him the most that he seems to come through for us. But that's not true, his presence is there all the time, it is more a matter of us opening ourselves up to hear his call. Listening to God does not take self-effort. Instead it takes a willingness to let go of your own feeble attempts to seek out God's answers. For it is only when we truly stop trying to do it all ourselves, and allow ourselves to fall into God's tranquility and peace that we are really able to grasp what he wants for us in life."

DANNY, age 17

Letters to God and Letters from God

This is another idea developed by Louise Spiker. In the case of letters to God or letters from God, the same idea is followed, except that the thoughts are developed in letter form, rather than in a dialogue. A person might write a long letter to God (much like a Dear Abby letter) in which the person explores his or her thoughts and feelings in some depth. Then the person could write a letter in which God responds (Dear Abby style) to the first letter. The key here is to be as faithful as possible to what you honestly think God would say. In the example above, a person would explore the same issue, but in letter form.

Meditation on Scripture

In meditating on scripture, a person reads a passage slowly and carefully, making notes on anything that gets his or her attention. Then, with that as background, the person will begin to meditate—reflect, think, ponder, free-associate—on what the scripture said. The person may want to do this mentally and write down only things that stand out. Or, the person may want to write the entire meditation on paper, carefully recording the thoughts and feelings that he or she becomes aware of. The meditation then takes on a life of its own, and the thoughts hook other thoughts. In a true meditation, the person does not know where the meditation will lead. The idea is that the scripture becomes the starting point for a journey.

Meditation on a Word or Image

The same process described above can be used in a variety of ways. The person may want to meditate on a key word, such as *love,* or *grace,* or *Jesus,* or *God*—or on an image, such as the cross in the sanctuary, a picture of Jesus' crucifixion, or a sunset. In this type of meditation, the image or word becomes the starting point. It leads the meditators beyond themselves to a reflection on some aspect of their relationship with God.

Creative Imaging

In creative imaging, a person uses an image to make God's presence more real. God is present with us all the time. God's presence is like the air we breathe and the sun—always there, but rarely in our awareness. With a little creativity, God's presence can be compared to something a person experiences all the time.

EXAMPLE: *Sun on the Body*

This imaging works best if the group members are outside and can feel the sun's rays on their skin or clothing. Have them close their eyes and feel the warmth of the sun's rays for a few moments. Then have them imagine that the rays of the sun are an expression of God's love for them. The warmth they feel is the warmth of God's love. Have them experience this for a few moments, then ask them to give a mental prayer to God, giving thanks for God's love.

EXAMPLE: *Wind on the Body*

This imaging technique is similar to the one above, in that it works best outdoors. Have the students feel the wind on their hair, faces, and skin. The amount of wind is not really important. A strong breeze can express God's power. A gentle breeze can express the caressing of God's presence. Have the group members experience the wind for a few moments, then have them think about the wind as an expression of God's Spirit. You might want to mention that the Old Testament word for *Spirit,* "ruah," also means *wind* and *breath.* Have them experience the wind as "ruah," as God's Spirit, or breath.

EXAMPLE: *Breathing*

The group can also link God's Spirit to breathing. Have the students close their eyes and become aware of their breathing. Have them feel the air going in and out of their bodies, giving life and oxygen. Link the breathing they are doing to the Hebrew word "ruah" for breath. Remind them that God "breathed" life into Adam in the creation story. Then have them imagine the breath they feel as the Spirit of God flowing into them, giving them life.

EXAMPLE: *Blood in Veins*

Have the group members feel the blood flowing through their veins. They can do this either by feeling their pulse or by becoming very still and feeling their hearts beat. They should be able to feel the flowing of blood through various parts of their bodies. Have them mentally image the blood flowing around and around in their bodies—giving them life. Then have them imagine God's love for them as that blood. Have them experience this image for a couple of minutes.

Contemplation

Contemplation, or "emptying" prayer, is more difficult than meditation. It is a learned skill that requires practice. Junior-high students find this difficult, but many in senior high find it helpful. In contemplation, one finds a place to be alone and tries to the best of his or her ability to go mentally blank. It is normal for this to be difficult. All kinds of random thoughts will come to mind—things we need to do, places we need to go.

Contemplation is best when it is coupled with breath work and journaling. Ask those who want to experience contemplation to take a few minutes for relaxation and breathing exercises. Then have them close their eyes and try to go blank. Explain that they are to *expect* difficulty with this exercise. Have them spend about thirty minutes trying to be empty. At the end of this exercise, ask them to journal what they experienced. They may have had physical sensations, seen lights or patterns behind their eyelids, had interesting thoughts pass through their minds.

Some contemplators like to read a passage of scripture or look at a symbol, such as a cross, just before they contemplate. For some, this is helpful as a point of focus. Contemplation is not for everyone, but some people, including teenagers, find it helpful. It can produce insights. At a minimum, it can be a very relaxing time.

Mystic Prayer

Mystic prayer is a form of meditation in which one deliberately tries to feel at one with God or God's creation. Many people have occasional paranormal experiences in which they feel at one with the universe or with God. Some people find looking at a sunset or some other work of nature to be helpful. Others turn contemplation into mystic prayer. The joys of mystic prayer are those rare moments when we feel a profound sense of "at-one-ment" with God or God's creation.

Dispositional Prayer

Dispositional prayer adds a whole new dimension to our spiritual life and the spiritual life of the young people we work with. In spiritual growth it is important to move beyond learning about God and to move toward ways we can have direct experiences of God. Like music and many forms of worship, dispositional prayer is more experiential than cognitive. It is learning to be in God's presence.

Some youth have a certain amount of initial resistance to dispositional prayer. The main reason seems to be that it is new and unfamiliar. Yet when they are exposed to many of the prayer forms in this chapter, they enjoy the activities and find them helpful in developing a sense of God's presence in their lives.

"There are varieties of services, but the same Lord."
FIRST CORINTHIANS 12:5

CHAPTER

4

WORSHIP

Several older members of the congregation swore that there never had been and never would be any "dancing" in Sunday morning worship. They didn't like the idea of young women parading around "half naked" in front of the congregation. It was too sexual.

When the youth worship committee heard this concern being voiced in some of the adult Sunday school classes, they decided to go ahead and keep the planned dance in their Sunday youth service, but they made some changes. In the bulletin it was called "liturgical movement." The five "dancers" were all modestly dressed and were all junior-high students.

The group was in front of the congregation three times during the worship service—once when they "signed" the scripture, once to do "liturgical movement" to a song, and once to provide interpretative movements to the creed. After the service, members of the congregation—including some of those who were skeptical—gave high praise to the beauty and power of the worship service. Since that first service, the youth group has continued to include liturgical dance in its worship leadership, including several times when it was invited to provide movement for special services.

The Cross

The highlight of junior-high camp that year was the worship committee's decision to portray the crucifixion by putting Marta on the cross. The focal point of the camp was Vesper Point, an outdoor worship area with a large wooden cross more than twenty feet tall. The committee had decided that on the last night of camp, they wanted to focus on the meaning of the crucifixion of Jesus in a powerful way.

At the beginning of the service, two adults put a tall ladder up to the cross, and Marta slowly climbed the ladder until she was in position. She never said a word, but the entire service took place as the sun set behind Marta on the cross. There was something about her silent presence there that gave a whole new meaning to the crucifixion that night. As the songs were sung, the scriptures read, and the skit acted out, Marta's silent witness bore testimony to what the service was about. Years later, people who were there that evening would still point to that service as one of the most memorable they had ever attended.

The Wall

The summer after the Berlin Wall came down, a group of senior-high students were discussing what to do in the closing worship for their retreat. They had been discussing the various walls that separate them from God and from one another. They decided to make their theme "The Wall."

Before the service, they constructed a large wall with butcher paper. The wall, when erected, was about ten feet high and more than twenty feet long. They had drawn bricks on it to make it look more real. At the beginning of the service the wall was put up in front of the worship area. It totally blocked the view of the cross.

At one point in the service, the two hundred young people present were invited to take markers and write on the wall things that separated them from God, from their families, and from others. Others spoke of the walls in their own lives. Later in the service, one person read Ephesians 1:14, in which Paul speaks of Christ tearing town the wall that separates us from God.

The participants were then invited to go up and take pieces of the wall, which represented barriers in their own lives, as a way of affirming God's power to overcome this obstacle. The image that many remembered years later was of the wall slowly crumbling and the cross emerging behind it. At the end, the wall was gone, the cross was visible, and each person had a piece of the wall to take home.

The Testimonies

The senior pastor confessed that he had never heard anything like it in his twenty years of ministry. As part of a Sunday morning worship service, four young people of the church had stood up and given testimonies about their faith. The testimonies were not dramatic or shocking. They revealed no great sins. But they were from the heart.

One after another, they had stood up before the congregation and shared their faith—what it was like to grow up in the congregation, what it was like to be new to the church and to be warmly received, how it felt to feel God's presence for the first time at a camp, what it was like to represent God and the church on a mission trip.

The pastor was supposed to follow this presentation with a brief sermon. After the last youth sat down, the pastor confessed that anything he could say would only detract from what had already been said.

"The Missing E"

The youth group was having a serious problem, and the youth fellowship worship committee had decided to deal with the issue in that evening's worship service. Some members of the group had dropped out and become inactive. Others felt unappreciated or unimportant. The committee wanted to use Paul's analogy of the body in First Corinthians 12, but the real breakthrough came when someone shared a poem called "The Missing E." The poem had one letter missing—there were no e's. The result was that the poem made no sense. Removing one letter made that much difference. This became the organizing idea for the service.

At the service, the group dealt head-on with the problem it was having. Several members shared what they were seeing and why it concerned them. First Corinthians 12 was read. Copies of the "Missing E" poem were passed out, and the group was invited to read it in silence. One member of the worship committee then invited everyone for a time of prayer at the altar rail.

On the altar were a paper sack and a basket. The worship leader stated that the key to solving the problem was in the sack. As the members finished a time of prayer and personal reflection, they were invited to look into the sack at God's solution to the problem, and then take one of the items from the basket.

When the group members came to the altar and looked into the bag, there were a variety of reactions. Some smiled, some laughed, others stared for several moments. A few cried. Each person then took one of the small objects in the basket and sat down.

In the sack, the group had placed an eight-inch circular mirror, as a reminder that each person there was both the source of the problem and the key to the solution. In the basket, each person picked up a small mirror with an "e" written on it. After that night's service, the "problem" the group had been experiencing went away. Years later, members of the group confessed that they still had their small mirrors with the "e."

The Bracelet

Everyone remembered the time when the youth group almost disbanded. Divisions and cliques had broken out. Some members stopped coming, and others openly announced that they didn't miss them. Attendance dropped from 80 down to fewer than 20. Several of the adult sponsors confessed they were discouraged and planned to stop working with the group. Even the youth minister confessed that for the first time in his ministry, he was considering whether his leaving might help the group.

When the youth council discussed the problem, it quickly decided that the most effective way to deal with the problem was in a youth fellowship worship service. The group valued worship. It was a setting where they would be the most likely to listen. The group planned the service and then sent a letter to all the young people in the church, inviting them to the worship and explaining briefly what was at stake.

That night, more than 100 young people and sponsors showed up. People who had not been seen in months were present. In the middle of the service, several people on the council shared their concern, their feelings, and their fears. Then they opened it up to the group. In the setting of worship, the group members begin to express their pain and frustration. Then the mood turned to confession. No one wanted to lose what they had in their youth group, yet everyone knew that the end was near. Then a member of the worship committee read a passage of scripture on covenant and invited the members of the group to make a covenant with God and with one another to make the group what it could be—to make a new beginning.

The group was invited to a time of prayer at the altar. Each member who were willing to make a new beginning was invited to put on a black and white bracelet that one of the adults had braided for the occasion. Black symbolized the death of what was. White symbolized rebirth. Three people got up and left the room. Others went to the altar to pray.

After several minutes, one person put on a bracelet. Then another. And another. During the next fifteen minutes, all the people who had stayed had put on bracelets. It was a turning point. The youth council was right. Worship was the right place to face the problem and recommit to solve it.

The characteristic that all the services above have in common is that they were totally planned and led by youth. Adults helped in the planning. But the key ideas and the leadership were given by young people. Those of us who work with youth know that youth groups can plan powerful services. Many of the most powerful and moving worship experiences I have ever had have taken place in services planned and led by youth. This chapter will explore how worship can be a vital part of our ministry with youth and a central part of teenagers' spiritual growth.

Definition of Worship

Worship has always been at the very center of what it means to be a Christian. Whenever the church has gathered, it has gathered to worship. There is no church and no Christian community without worship. In the same way, our spiritual growth is anchored in worship. Worship renews our spirit. It strengthens and feeds us spiritually. In worship, we are comforted, strengthened, challenged, forgiven, fed, and educated.

In our work with youth, especially in our attempts to help teens grow in their relationship with God, worship lies at the very center of what we do. It is not just another tool for our work with youth. In many ways, worship is the very heart and soul of all we are about.

There is a wide variety of definitions for worship. One seminary textbook on worship traces the word back to the old Anglo-Saxon word for *worth*. In this sense, worship is an activity through which we ascribe worth to God. The current version of *The American Heritage Dictionary* gives three definitions that explain the meaning of Christian worship:

1. Reverent love and respect;
2. A set of ceremonies or prayer by which this devotion is expressed;
3. Love of or devotion to a person or thing.

There are several key components to Christian worship. Each is important and conveys an important dimension of worship.

Christian Worship Is Corporate

Worship is distinct and different from private devotions. An individual can pray, read scripture, sing songs, or do many of the activities that are done in worship. But it is not worship unless the community is gathered. Worship is, by definition, corporate. Worship is an act of the community, not of the individual. It doesn't need to involve the whole community. A church can have several worship services, including one at the evening youth fellowship meeting. But to be worship, the community needs to be present in some form.

Christian Worship Is God Directed

Even though worship is a human activity, it is directed at God. God is the object of worship. It differs from many human activities in that it does not focus on us. Rather, worship's focus is on God—on who God is, on how God is with us, on what God calls us to be.

Christian Worship Is Christ-Centered

Christian worship, as distinct from other forms of worship, is centered in the revelation of God in Christ. It is not just God who is the focus. It is God as revealed in Jesus, whom we proclaim to be the Christ. Our worship has a particular understanding of who God is. It focuses on how God is revealed in the life and ministry of Jesus.

Christian Worship Is Biblically Based

The scriptures are the ultimate source of our understanding of God and Jesus. Worship is anchored in the biblical revelation of God. The heart of any worship service is the reading of scripture and the contemporary proclamation of its message in some way. Worship cannot be cut off from the scriptures. If it is, it is cut adrift from its anchor.

Christian Worship Is Context Sensitive

Worship is not only anchored in the historical revelation of God in the Bible. It is also context sensitive. Worship is always done by a particular group of people in a particular time and place. A worshiping congregation has very specific needs and concerns, and worship seems to address these needs.

Youth worship speaks to the needs of youth. It addresses the concerns and issues of youth. It is appropriate to youth. As such, it will be different in some respects from worship geared to adults. In the same way, if a worship service is geared to the whole congregation on Sunday morning, it must include the concerns and issues of youth to be authentic worship.

Christian Worship Is Participatory

Worship is not a spectator sport. It is literally *liturgy*—"the work of the people." Worship is, by its very nature, participatory. Youth worship should involve youth in planning, in leading, and those who are not leading should be actively involved in whatever is going on. Just as adults cannot "do" worship for youth, youth worship leaders (even those who lead) cannot "do" worship for the congregation. Everyone present must be actively involved.

Christian Worship Is Spirit Led

Ultimately, there is a mystery about worship. It is a human activity. We plan it. We lead it. Yet the best worship experiences happen when the worship becomes more than we planned. There are those moments when the Spirit of God seems to take over and move within a group. It may happen in the planning process or in the worship service itself. It is helpful to remember that ultimately, the worship service is God's, not ours. And it is at its best when we get out of the Spirit's way and let the Spirit move within the service.

Involving Youth in Sunday Morning Services

Participation in the main Sunday morning worship services is and will continue to be the main worship issue for worship with youth. Sunday morning is when the community gathers. For most churches, it may be the only time during the week when the church gathers as a total congregation. If the young people of the congregation are not vitally involved in the main Sunday morning services, they are cut off from the congregation's worship as a total body. We may provide other opportunities for youth to worship, but there is no substitute for participation in the Sunday morning services.

Young people are a part of the congregation. They are not just "the future of the church." Although well intentioned, the real implication of this oft-quoted comment is that they are "not the present of the church." Nothing could be further from the truth. Not only do young people benefit from a worship that is sensitive to their needs, but they also have a lot to contribute to worship.

In many local churches, the teenagers are marginalized in Sunday morning worship. They are not included in any meaningful way. The sermons do not speak to them and their concerns. The music is alien to them. They are asked to be passive participants in an activity that is alien to them. Yet in many other congregations, they are involved in dynamic ways. We need to find ways for the services we offer to speak to youth as well as ways for youth to become involved in the services as leaders.

Involving Youth in the Service as Participants

The pastor's relationship with the youth of the congregation is a crucial factor. Young people are relational. If they feel as if they know the person who is speaking, they will be more attentive and involved. If they feel that the pastor is a stranger, they will have little reason for focusing on what the pastor says. What happens outside the pulpit affects the way what is said from the pulpit is received.

There are things the pastor or worship leader can do that will help teenagers feel they belong. Most of these things are very simple, yet collectively, they can make a difference:

1. **Refer to youth and youth concerns in the sermons.** If the speaker is knowledgeable about the young people of the congregation and community, their issues and concerns, this material can be brought into the morning message. Letting a youth Sunday school class know that the morning message will refer to their mission trip, or something that happened in the local middle school, or someone they know, can have a dramatic effect. Many teenagers expect that worship and the morning sermon will contain nothing that relates to their world. If the opposite is true, if they come with the expectation that the person bringing the morning message is likely to refer to something they can relate to, the results can be dramatic.

2. **Use illustrations that relate to the world your youth live in.** The pastor must speak to the entire congregation. Young people don't expect the pastor to focus exclusively on their concerns every week, but they are as much a part of the congregation as the older members of the church. Illustrative material needs to come from a variety of sources. An illustration that relates to the world youth live in can carry great power—a popular song, a recent movie, a TV show, an event

in the community that affects youth, an example from the life of a youth—each of these can capture the attention of teenage members of the congregation.

3. **Sing songs that youth can relate to.** Many contemporary denominational hymnals contain songs that young people can relate to and enjoy. Morning worship also occasionally can incorporate songs that are meaningful to them. If there is a guitar player in the congregation, this can add a whole new dimension to singing and to worship. Youth music does not need to replace the music the congregation is currently using, but it can supplement it in meaningful ways. Many of the older members of the congregation also enjoy contemporary music. Many of the songs used in youth ministry ("Pass It On"; "They'll Know We Are Christians") have been around for nearly thirty years. The baby boomers in the congregation probably know many of these songs as well as the teenagers do. Other more recent music, such as that by Amy Grant and other contemporary artists, can add much to worship.

4. **Address youth concerns in prayers and liturgy.** There is no reason why the prayers and liturgy used in worship can't address the issues and concerns of youth in meaningful ways. The pastoral prayer can make a reference or two to the concerns of the younger members of the congregation. A responsive liturgy, affirmation of faith, or prayer of confession can include relevant issues and concerns.

The basic issue in each of these areas is sensitivity—being sensitive to a whole segment of the congregation and attempting to make worship "youth friendly" and relevant to their legitimate concerns and issues.

"Ever since I was old enough to stay awake through church, the main event for that hour would be counting those who didn't quite make it. 'Big church' is what people call it, simply because it is geared toward the big people or elders of our church. How can we as youth feel a part of the sermon if it is so boring that we end up using the hour as an extension of our Sunday morning sleep? We really could add to the service if we spiced up the youth choir songs by adding a little clapping or motion that would make us feel welcome. If the church was geared toward the family, then all ages would attend, and involvement in the church would grow, including youth."

LESLIE, age 15

Involving Youth in the Service as Leaders

We also can do a lot of things to involve young people in the leadership of worship. They have much to offer. With few exceptions, there is nothing an adult can do in worship that a youth cannot do. They can:

* *Serve as Ushers and Greeters.* Many churches have found that young people make excellent ushers. They can greet, hand out bulletins, help seat people, take the offering, and so on. The concern here is the same as it would be with adults—that the people functioning in this role need to be friendly and have a certain amount of training so that they know what to do.

* *Read Scripture.* Many teenagers also make excellent readers. Not every youth can read well, but many can read as well as any adult. There will be a certain amount of natural fear the first couple of times a young person (or anyone else) reads before the whole congregation. But this will pass with experience. You may want to help young people get over this fear by having them practice reading the passage out loud from the pulpit before the service.

* *Present the Children's Message.* Many young people have an innate ability to relate to younger children. Many have younger brothers and sisters and know how to effectively communicate with children. They may need help with ideas, and an adult worship leader may need to sit with them and the children. But in many instances, the chemistry between a youth and the children can enhance the children's message.

* *Serve as Liturgists.* If the congregation uses lay liturgists in the morning worship, it would be good to use a young person in this role. There are probably some in most congregations who could do a very effective job of leading prayers, responsive readings, and affirmations of faith.

* *Sing in a Youth Choir.* Most adults love it when the youth of the church sing. In some churches, this is done occasionally. In others, it is done on a regular basis. If the church has multiple services, the youth might provide music for one of these. If this is the case, it is helpful for the youth choir to be seen occasionally in the other services.

* *Serve as Soloists and Musicians.* Many of the youth are trained musicians. They sing in school choirs, perform in orchestras and bands. These are talents that would enhance the Sunday morning worship services for many congregations.

* *Provide Liturgical Movement or Signing.* Many congregations have come to appreciate and value the contribution that liturgical movement or signing can make to a worship service. Many adults would be intimidated to do this in front of others. But young people often enjoy the opportunity. Signing a prayer, song, or scripture; providing liturgical movement to go along with part of the service; including a sacred dance as a part of the service—each of these can provide a powerful and moving addition to a service of worship.

* *Serve as Acolytes.* In many congregations elementary children and teenagers help with worship by being acolytes. Their duties can include lighting the candles at the beginning of the service, bringing the offering forward, extinguishing the

candles at the end of the service, and so on. Junior-high students are especially fond of providing this service.

The Key: Working with the Pastor

The key to involving youth in the morning worship is, and will continue to be, the pastor. In most of our congregations, the responsibility for worship resides with the pastor. If we want to involve more young people in worship, we will need to work closely with the pastor.

In my own ministry, I spent twelve years as the pastor in charge before going into full-time youth ministry. As a pastor, I had a wide variety of opportunities to involve youth in worship. As a member of a church staff, I need to work with the person in charge of worship.

Youth Sunday Services

Even though we can do a lot to make the regular morning worship more youth friendly, there is still a lot to be said for occasional "Youth Sunday" worship services. The basic idea for Youth Sunday has been around for a long time. These occasional services are not primarily for the youth. They are services in which the youth of the church—as a group—lead morning worship for the congregation.

There seem to be two basic models of this service currently in use: the "everything but" model and the "total" model. In the "everything but" model, the young people provide everything but the sermon. They sing, read the scriptures, present the children's message, lead all the liturgy, prayers, creeds, and so on. Then an adult (the pastor or youth minister) preaches the sermon.

In the other model, the young people provide the entire service. Adults help in the planning of the service, but the teenagers lead the service from start to finish, including the sermon. There is a lot to be said for this latter model. Young people have a lot to say. In many of our churches, there are several who can craft and present an excellent sermon. I personally prefer having several youth share this responsibility. Three or four can collectively speak to a topic or theme. This takes the pressure off any one youth. If a particular presentation is weak, the others can carry it. The morning message can be presented in a variety of ways: mini-sermon, personal testimonies, skits, song, and so on.

Another issue to be dealt with is whether to use the regular order of worship. There is a lot to be said for changing the order. A creative tension exists in the unexpected. But for many congregations, following the normal order is easier, both on the youth leading and on the congregation. If the normal order is followed, different youth can take the various parts of the service. It is easy to use 15 to 20 youth in this way. Others can sing in a choir or provide special music.

It's helpful if the youth of the church take on this service as a group and see it as a "service" they are providing to the congregation. Their service needs to be carefully planned and rehearsed. It's helpful to rehearse the various parts of the service individually. You can meet and work with those doing the children's message, the sermon, and the prayers. They may want to stand in the pulpit and practice to get the feel of what they will be doing. It's also helpful to have a dress rehearsal—to run through the service from beginning to end. This lets them know who they follow, what they will do, and who follows them. It helps calm fears, performance anxiety, and makes things go more smoothly at the service.

Youth Worship on Sunday Evening

Even if the youth are actively and meaningfully engaged in the congregation's morning worship, and also provide occasional Youth Sunday services for the congregation, there is still a need for them to plan and lead their own worship services. There is a limit to what can be done for youth in a worship service when the focus is on the congregation as a whole.

Why Youth Need Their Own Worship Service

In most of our churches, the ideal place for a service specifically designed to address the needs and concerns of youth is the Sunday evening youth fellowship. In that setting the entire worship service can be custom-designed for youth. Both "The Missing E" and "The Bracelet" services mentioned earlier were created for this setting. Neither of these services could have been presented on Sunday morning, yet each played a crucial role in the life of its respective youth group.

Young people learn more about worship by planning and leading worship than they can ever learn by sitting in a service. Youth fellowship worship service can address specific needs of the group week after week. In many youth groups, worship has become a regular part of youth fellowship. The model suggested here is for a 30-minute service, planned and led by youth each Sunday.

A Model for Youth Fellowship

The model suggested here was developed by young people and adults at a senior-high summer camp, and it has continued to evolve over the years. It has been adopted by many youth fellowships to be used as a part of their regular weekly Sunday evening format. It allows for a lot of flexibility and creativity, yet its basic structure is simple and consistent.

The model is based on a worship committee of youth and adults who meet before the service and plan the worship. The basic order remains fairly consistent. But the theme and content will shift from week to week, depending upon any needs the worship committee is aware of. Occasionally, the committee will change the worship for a special service, such as a "Catacomb Service" or the Lord's Supper.

An Order of Worship

Gathering

What happens before the service and as it starts is important. If worship is new to the group, or if the group has trouble focusing, the members need to be reminded that they are making a transition from the previous activity to worship. They can be taught an "attitude of worship," or an "attitude of prayer." This attitude involves both reverence for God and respect for the older people in the group for whom worship is important.

The setting is also important. If possible, make a physical transition into a different room. If the church sanctuary or chapel is available and helps to create a worshipful atmosphere, you may want to use it. If the room leaves something to be desired, you may want to turn off the lights and have the service in candlelight. This can have a very powerful effect. Music should be playing as the group enters. A pianist or guitarist, if available, could provide music, or you may want to use taped music. Another possibility is to sing the first song as you enter the room. This will immediately involve the group in the act of worship. Avoid a lull. If there is downtime before the service begins, you may lose the group's attention.

Opening Songs

Music can be used to set the mood of worship. We usually use three songs. The first is loud and relatively lively. This brings the group on board together. The second song is more moderate, and the last is soft and slow. The cumulative effect is to have the group focus together and then slowly calm down. If your group already has reverence for worship, you may want to use only mellow songs. Use young people as song leaders. Volunteers who are not part of the leadership team can lead the music. If possible, have different people in this role each week.

Opening Prayer

Ask one of the youth to open with prayer. This should be short and, if possible, introduce the team of the worship service. You might want to use some of the prayer forms mentioned in the chapter on active prayer, such as the "say with me prayers."

Scripture Presentation

Ask an individual or a group to present the scripture. Reading is only one way a scripture passage can be presented. It can be acted out, mimed, paraphrased, reverse paraphrased, and so on. If the passage is short, reading it may be best. If it is a story, a dramatic presentation of the text might be appropriate. Variety is helpful. Teenagers are more inclined to listen to the passage if the approaches vary from week to week.

The Devotion

The devotion, or the "message" part of the service, can be presented in a wide variety of ways through: *testimonies, having one or more persons say what the passage means to them,* or *dramas or skits*. There are also books that contain prewritten devotions that can be adapted. The most powerful devotions, though, are the ones created by the group for a specific situation, such as the "The Missing E" and "The Bracelet."

Response

It's helpful not to limit the message to the worship leadership team. Following the message, you may want to open up the meeting to the group as a whole and invite comments and thoughts. At times, no one will have anything to add. At other times, the most powerful words spoken may be by someone in the group.

Joys and Concerns

Invite the group to a time of sharing of joys, concerns, and prayer requests. One person can introduce this to the group and suggest a sentence to be said after each concern is voiced. You might want to use "Hear our prayer, O Lord," or "This is our prayer," or some other appropriate form. This response lets the group know when one concern is over and it is okay to give the next. It's also helpful if the person leading the joys and concerns will repeat each joy or concern first, as in, "A concern for Tim's mother, who is in the hospital. Hear our prayer, O Lord." This helps make sure that everyone hears each concern.

Altar Prayer Time, or Lord's Prayer

In many of our churches, we lost the opportunity to pray at the altar rail when we lost our evening services. Many young people find a time of silent prayer at the altar rail to be especially valuable. After the concerns, joys, and prayer requests have been voiced, ask the leader to invite the group to come to the altar for a time of prayer. Dim the lights if you have not already done so. If possible, have soft music (taped or live) playing in the background. Don't rush this part of the service, but encourage group members to take the time they need.

"For me, worship is one of the most important parts of my spirituality. It is a time when I can focus solely on God and my faith. The part of worship that is the most meaningful to me is altar time. My prayers at the altar seem to be more inspired and more directed. It's as if I'm connected to God through the songs, prayers, and scriptures of the worship. Sharing a worship experience with others helps me to feel enlightened in the Holy Spirit, therefore my prayer at the altar reflects the love and fulfillment I have experienced in worship."

NICOLE, *age 16*

An alternative to ending the joys and concerns with altar prayer time is to simply close by asking the group to recite the Lord's Prayer. This allows the group members to end the prayer time as a group and clearly signals that prayer time is over and the next part of the service is about to begin.

Closing Circle (Prayer, Song, Benediction)

When the group has finished praying, ask the members to form a circle by linking arms. In large groups, you may want them to form rows or simply reach out on either side for someone's hand. The closing circle can have three parts. A youth can close with a brief prayer. You can sing a short, simple song that everyone knows, and the group can end with a benediction:

> The LORD bless you and keep you;
> the LORD make his face to shine upon you, and be gracious to you;
> the LORD lift up his countenance upon you, and give you peace.
> —Numbers 6:24-26

Some youth groups will vary this benediction by accentuating the word *you*, or by looking at a different person each time the word *you* is said, or by pointing to a different person each time. Encourage the group to "get some hugs" after the service.

Creating a Devotional

Even though there are several good devotional books available with meditations that can be adapted for youth worship, the best devotions are those that are created by the group for the situation. A simple procedure for creating a devotion which ensures that the devotional is both biblically faithful and appropriate to the situation was developed in the summer camp setting. It uses the following steps:

1. **Exegete the passage.** It's easy to proof-text scripture. Young people find it easy to have some point they want to communicate, and then ask for some scripture to back it up. The trouble is that this is *isogesis*—reading into the scripture what we want it to say. This does violence to the scripture and is inappropriate for Christian worship.

   A better approach is *exegesis*—to read out of the text what it is saying. This is relatively simple for most passages of scripture. An adult can help a group of youth:
   (a) read the passage;
   (b) decide what its theme or topic is;
   (c) and then decide what it says about the topic.

   This is the starting point for the service. Everything else is built on what we understand the scripture to be saying, not vice versa.

2. **Exegete the group.** The next step is to exegete the group, much as you did the passage:

   * What is going on in our group right now?
   * What are the issues and concerns we are struggling with?
   * And, in particular, where do the issues of our group meet the issues raised by the scripture?

   At times, a group may want to reverse steps one and two, in order to consider a particular issue the group is dealing with. In this case, the group might want to examine what is going on in the group and determine the issue. Then the group can look for appropriate scriptures that deal with the same or related issues. If the steps are reversed, it is important to make sure that the texts found are used for what they really say, not for what the group wants them to say.

3. **Decide what to say based on what *this* passage says to *this* group at *this* time.** Once the first two steps are done, the next step is to decide what to say to the group. Three concerns are central here:
   (a) the message will be based on the scripture;
   (b) it is appropriate to the group it is being presented to; and
   (c) it is appropriate to that moment.

4. **Decide how you will do this.** Once you have decided what it is you want to say, based on the first three steps, you can decide how you will communicate this message. You may want to use a skit, testimonies, or an idea from a book. Once you know where you're going, it is relatively easy to decide how to get there.

5. **Decide who will do this.** This is the step that many young people want to take first. The problem is that if several people have strong opinions about wanting to do particular things before the group decides—as a group—what it wants to do, there is a danger that the worship will be ill focused. Worship is not a showcase for individual talents. Our talents are subservient to the service itself. Having this step follow the previous four steps guarantees that when a person volunteers to lead the worship, he or she will lead the worship that the committee has planned.

6. **Plan the rest of the service around this message.** Once the devotion is planned, the rest of the service follows quickly and naturally. Prayers, songs, and other parts of the service are chosen to fit the devotion and the theme of the service.

Communion

Communion, the Lord's Supper, needs to be a regular part of youth worship. Unfortunately, most youth groups do not have an ordained person working with the group. But this is an excellent opportunity to involve the pastor in the group's worship. There are people in the typical youth group who are not members of the church or who may not come on Sunday morning. Regular, monthly communion allows the sacrament to be a part of the life of the group, and the pastor to connect with the group in a meaningful and appropriate way.

Worship on Trips and Special Occasions

Camps, trips, and retreats provide excellent opportunities for the group to worship together, so that worship becomes an important part of the shared experience on the trip. Camps and retreats are often in beautiful natural settings. An evening service at sunset can set a wonderful mood for worship. Worship times can be brief, but also can be good times for the whole group to focus together as a community.

Because young people are open to new ideas, they can also be a conduit for introducing new and exciting worship experiences into the congregation. Adults expect the youth to do things that are different. The worshiping congregation is more tolerant when the youth do new and innovative things than it often is of the pastor.

Special occasions provide wonderful opportunities for the youth to lead the entire congregation in worship. Many congregations find the following special occasions especially appropriate.

Easter Sunrise Service

In countless congregations, the youth of the church provide the Easter sunrise service. The youth can plan and lead the service, which can then be followed by a fellowship time, with breakfast at the church or an area restaurant. The youth choir could perform, skits could be done, testimonies could be shared. The service can be brief, but is best if it begins in twilight and reaches its climax just as the sun cracks over the horizon.

Good Friday Tenebrae Service

The Good Friday Tenebrae service is built around a series of readings that retell the story of the last night in the life of Jesus. Many churches have discovered that the youth of the church can provide the readers and the music for this service. Tenebrae is a kind of reverse candlelight service that has a lot of emotional power and can focus the congregation's attention on the meaning of Lent.

Contemporary Hymn Sing

Young people are often the first to learn contemporary Christian music. Many of the songs they sing on retreats, at camps, and at their evening fellowship are songs the congregation would also appreciate. The baby-boomers and younger generations were raised on many of the same songs. The youth could introduce these songs into morning worship or—on special occasions—provide a contemporary hymn sing.

Catacomb Worship

Catacomb worship is an emotionally powerful form of worship that has become popular among many youth groups in recent years. This worship form seeks to recreate what it was like to worship in the early Christian community. There were no Bibles or songbooks. Often, the leaders of the community were in prison or had been killed. The basic idea behind the worship service is that we—our memories, our experiences, our faith—are the basic resource for worship.

*The catacomb service is a candlelight service.

*Find a room that the group can fit into, but in which they will be cramped. Use votive candles to form a cross on the floor in the center of the room.

*As the group enters the room, have someone start a song the group knows.

*As each song ends, someone else starts another, or calls out the title of a song so that another person can start it. The group sings as much of each song as it remembers, and can sing as long as it wants.

*Then someone asks if a person present will lead the opening prayer. Do the same for joys and concerns.

When it is time to read scripture, the leader mentions that there is no Bible and invites people to share scripture passages that are important to them. The scripture can be quoted exactly, or summarized. Someone may just remember a story in brief form.

After the scripture, someone invites the people to share what they think God might say to this group at this moment in time. Anyone who wants to share does so. If possible, the group then has communion, singing softly in the background as communion is served. The service then ends with a closing prayer and everyone departs the room in silence.

Two things are important in doing a catacomb service. Although it appears that the service is leaderless, make sure that people who know what is supposed to happen are ready to facilitate the worship. Individuals need to be prepared to start songs, share prayer requests, scripture passages, and the Word of the Lord. No one wants to be first in any of these, but if a few can break the ice and share, the whole group will often follow. One or more leaders need to facilitate the service and verbally ask people to pray or share at appropriate times.

The other thing that is important for a catacomb service is to carefully explain to the group before you enter the room what you are doing and how it will work. Set expectations high. The more seriously they take the service, the more they will get out of it.

A "Messageless" Prayer Service

A messageless service follows the same order as the youth fellowship worship model shared above, except that there will be no devotion or message. Prayer becomes the focus of the service. The group sings, shares joys and concerns, has altar prayer time, then closes. This form of worship is especially appropriate when time is limited, when someone forgets to plan the service, or just as a break from the regular order.

The Worship Committee

Many of the worship services mentioned in this chapter were planned by a youth worship committee. Worship does not just happen. It needs to be carefully planned and led—by the youth. One of the best ways to accomplish this on a regular basis is to have a standing worship committee. This may be a part of your youth council structure, or it may exist separately.

Many churches have a representative from each grade and an adult volunteer to form the group that is responsible for seeing that worship is planned. The committee members are not to lead all the worship services themselves. Their responsibility is twofold:

1. to plan worship; and
2. to recruit others to help them lead the worship experiences.

The adult acts as a facilitator or enabler. The adult facilitates the process and helps the group think through what it wants to say. The young people provide the basic ideas and the up-front leadership. The adult can be very instrumental in giving support, sparking ideas, and helping the group prepare for the service.

Worship is central to spiritual growth. Young people need to be included in the worship of the congregation, yet they also need opportunities to create their own services that focus on their needs. I hope this chapter has given you some ideas you can use with your group as you develop its spirituality in worship.

"Continue in what you have learned and firmly believed, knowing from whom you learned it."

SECOND TIMOTHY 3:14

5 SPECIAL TECHNIQUES AND RESOURCES

Bible study, prayer, and worship have always been the core tools for spiritual growth. This has remained unchanged for several thousand years and is likely to remain unchanged. But these three are not the only tools for spiritual growth at our disposal. There are a lot of different ways to foster spiritual development. This chapter will briefly explore ten of these techniques and resources. Books have been written on most of these topics. The concern here is to note how each of these techniques can be used to enhance our relationship with God and our spiritual growth.

Spiritual Mentoring

Anyone who works with youth is a spiritual mentor. Young people naturally look up to the adults who work with them as role models and mentors. When adults work with youth, this is a mentor relationship. But there is a second, more restricted sense in which spiritual mentoring is used.

Through the ages, Christians who have wanted to grow in their faith have sought out others to help in their spiritual journey. Among peers, these are often referred to as spiritual friends, spiritual pals, or what Morton Kelsey has called "companions on the inner way."

A spiritual mentor is an adult who agrees to work with one or more youth on a one-to-one basis. The content of the meetings is the spiritual journey. The mentor helps the young person by asking the age-old question, "How goes it with your spirit?" This is sometimes called spiritual counseling. It is similar to a counseling relationship, except that the content is explicitly spiritual, rather than psychological, and the purpose is to enhance the relationship, rather than troubleshoot a problem. The mentor and the student can process scripture, work through a book, discuss life experiences, explore issues, or do whatever seems appropriate to the relationship.

In the broader sense, we have this relationship with each youth we work with. Or, looking at it from the other direction, a youth should be able to see each of the adults who work with the youth program as a spiritual mentor. Being intentional about this aspect of our relationship can enhance our ministry to young people.

Journaling

Journaling is a way to keep a record of our relationship with God. It involves writing down one's thoughts, feelings, and experiences in relation to God. Journaling has already been discussed as a prayer technique, but it also can be used as a spiritual growth tool. Within youth ministry, there are three approaches to journaling that are helpful:

* *The Diary Approach*

In the diary approach, the person keeping the spiritual journal writes entries, just as one would in a diary. The difference is in the content of the diary. Instead of being random thoughts and feelings or a log of the day's experiences, the journal keeper focuses on those things that seem to have some relationship with his or her spiritual journey.

* *Letters to God*

The journal keeper may want to write letters to God in a "Dear Abby" fashion. Instead of writing to a columnist for advice, the letters are written to God. In this way, the writer is free to pour out his or her inner thoughts and feelings and lift them to God in prayer form.

* *Dialogues with God*

The journal keeper may want to enter into a dialogue with God in written form. The writer would write a Dear Abby type entry, then add what he or she believes God would say in reply.

In the following chapter on retreats, you will find several examples of journaling used as a spiritual growth tool.

Spiritual Autobiographies

Normally, we do not take time to stop and reflect on the presence of God in our lives and our spiritual journey. The purpose of a spiritual autobiography is to take a look at our lives and see where God has had an effect. In a spiritual autobiography, a person may write on such topics as:

1. My earliest awareness or experience of God
2. The moment I felt closest to God
3. The time when God felt most real
4. A time when I felt distant from God
5. Important events that have shaped my faith
6. Important people in my spiritual formation
7. Where I am right now in my relationship with God
8. One thing missing in my relationship with God is . . . .

In addition to writing responses to various topics, there are several other inventive ways to create spiritual autobiographies that work well with youth.

* Written Autobiography

One alternative is to write your life story in paragraph form, focusing on the issues that have affected your relationship with God and your spiritual journey. The eight topics above, and others like them, can be used to guide the writer.

* Life Graph

For those who are more visual, a life graph is a possibility. A life graph looks like an electrocardiogram, with a jagged line going up and down. The person making the graph draws his or her life, with all its ups and downs, then goes back and adds words or symbols to note particular events or people. In this form, both the personal life and the spiritual life of the person are shown on the same line. After the graph is completed, the person can verbally share his or her spiritual journey, using the graph as an aid.

* Dual Graph

A dual graph is exactly the same as the graph above, with one exception. Two graphs are created, one on top of the other. One graph narrates the person's personal life. The other narrates the spiritual journey. The dual graph is especially helpful in showing how our personal lives affect our spiritual journeys, and vice versa.

* Road Map

Junior-high students are especially fond of the road-map approach. In this approach, a person's life is depicted as a road, with dead ends, under-construction signs, accidents, potholes, and hazards.

* Pipe-cleaner Graph

Junior highs also can use a pipe cleaner to make a graph. By bending the wire up and down, the highs and lows of the spiritual journey can be depicted. In this approach, there is usually nothing written down. The young person simply explains what the ups and downs on the wire mean.

The key to all these approaches is interpretation, rather than presentation. The spiritual autobiography becomes a means of opening up. The sharing, and the discussion that follows, are what is important. In small groups, you can have the group members ask questions about the autobiography after the person shares. This will help the group better understand the biography, and help the writer to see things in his or her life that otherwise may be missed.

Dreamwork

Throughout the history of our faith, dreams have been seen as one of the ways in which God speaks to us. Even in a psychological approach, it is clear that our dreams are important and can help us understand what is going on in our lives. Dreams that have religious symbolism or seem to convey some important message can be very relevant to our walk with

God. Taking the time to understand a dream, whether in a personal journal or in a small-group setting, can be helpful. In the bibliography, you will find listed a book that contains more than thirty dreamwork approaches helpful in understanding the religious significance of dreams.

Music

Music has the power to speak to the soul. It is not accidental that music is a crucial part of worship. Young people also find music and singing powerful spiritual disciplines, in and of themselves. Music ties directly to the emotions. It has the power to evoke memories. Music and group singing should be a vital part of any youth program. Many excellent music resources are currently available.

Songs, by Songs & Creations, is probably the most complete songbook currently available. Group Publishing also has a songbook available, as does Abingdon Press. Both of these have compact disks and tapes available, which make the songs easy to learn and sing along with, especially for groups that may not have someone to play the guitar or piano.

Most of these songs have a few simple chords, and one strumming pattern works for nearly all of them. It is not unusual for a youth to learn how to play the guitar well enough to lead group singing in a few weeks. This will add a dimension to youth worship and to the spiritual tone of group gatherings.

Fasting

Fasting has been called "the forgotten discipline" and is rarely discussed in youth circles, though some groups will have an Easter vigil fast or a fast on New Year's Eve. Historically, fasting serves several purposes. Some youth leaders use fasting to heighten sensitivity to world hunger and poverty issues. Others have used it as a tool for self-denial and discipline. But the original purpose of fasting was quite different. Fasting originally was linked to prayer, especially meditation and contemplation. Those who fast claim that it clears the mind so that it can focus more intently. There is some evidence that fasting causes biochemical changes in the body.

In youth work, fasting needs to be used with great care. Young bodies are developing and growing rapidly. They have special nutritional needs. The literature on fasting recommends that youth never fast longer than twenty-four hours and that they be allowed to drink fluids (especially juice). It is also important to process and debrief the experience.

If fasting is used as a tool for spiritual growth, it needs to be used for a purpose, and the purpose needs to be clearly stated. Otherwise, young people will not understand the difference between a spiritual fast and dieting to lose weight.

Depth Discipleship Training

A common complaint by many young people is that they are not challenged. Sunday school is "boring." They are not learning anything new. The list goes on and on. Though we need a healthy skepticism about some of these statements, we also need to listen to the concern behind the words. Many are not sufficiently challenged by the ministry we currently offer them. They are ready for more. This probably will not be true for all the youth in your church, or even the majority, but it will be true for some.

We need to provide challenging, depth experiences for these young people. They are ready for intentional discipleship training. Depth discipleship training will be different from our other youth work. We are not looking for numbers. We are not seeking to sell the idea so that we can attract as many people as possible. Depth training, such as the Youth Edition of *Disciple*, Covenant Discipleship Groups, Peer Counseling, or Chrysalis Weekends, need to be offered to those who are ready for it and have expressed an interest. Groups need to be small, so that each person can have individual attention. These groups also need to be long-term. It takes time to work through spiritual growth issues or to take a youth to a new level of spiritual growth.

In addition to the programs currently available that provide opportunities for depth discipleship training, you may want to create your own study or format.

Recently in our church, we created a new Sunday school class for senior-high youth who felt they were not challenged by the traditional classes. They requested a class where the answers were not assumed, where they could ask difficult theological questions, such as "How do I really know there is a God?"; "How do I really know that anything I am taught about our faith is true?"; "What really makes Jesus better than Mohammed or Buddha?" They were asking for what in seminary is called systematic theology.

We created the new class, hoping that the three or four who had requested it (and perhaps a few more) would be motivated enough to attend on a regular basis. Much to everyone's surprise, we have been averaging thirty each Sunday. The class members are even beginning to bring in their friends from high school to attend the class.

Sometimes this type of training is reserved for the leadership "core group." There is a danger in this. Those who are ready for depth training and those who have the inclination and the ability to be leaders may or may not be the same people.

One of the special issues that arises in the midst of youth ministry, and especially with depth discipleship training, is the question of how to handle calls to ministry. It is a privilege to be there with young people when this issue arises. If we are uncomfortable with the topic or feel that it raises issues we are not adequately trained to deal with, we can request the assistance of the pastor or someone else on the staff of the church.

Our role is to neither push nor hinder, but to gently encourage the young person to work through his or her feelings and thoughts. If the person feels called by God, we can affirm this without burdening the young person with the thought that this decision is for life. The call may take a new direction in the future, or it may turn out to be something else entirely. What we affirm is that, *at this moment,* the young person feels led in a certain direction and is making a certain commitment.

Mission and Service

Anyone who has been on a mission trip or in a mission experience with young people knows the potential of these experiences for our spiritual growth. In spiritual autobiographies, mission trips rank high as moments of feeling close to God. Many of us have experienced testimonies of youth who say that the most powerful spiritual growth experiences in their lives have been connected to mission trips and service activities. Spiritual growth is tied to mission and service. Involving young people in mission experiences can bring them closer to God. They can see Christ in their neighbor. God is not just experienced through the Bible, prayer, and worship. God is very much at work in the world, and involving young people in mission work can help bring the God of the scriptures to life.

It is important to debrief any mission experience for its spiritual growth dimension. Seeing any mission experience as an opportunity for spiritual growth, and taking the time to debrief it, can add a whole new dimension to the spirituality of the young people we work with.

Small Groups

There is a historic link between spiritual growth and the intensive small-group experience. John Wesley organized the early Methodists into classes. Young Life, Campus Crusade, and other groups that are intentional about spiritual growth and discipleship have used the small group as one of their primary tools.

"Being in small groups has had an affect on me, because the pressures of 'pretending you don't care' go away. In Sunday school the majority of the class carries on private conversations during the lesson, whereas in small groups everyone settles down and takes the topic to heart. In large groups people tend to lose interest and miss the message entirely, while others who have a desire to learn are distracted by the constant stirring of the person beside them. I have found that small groups provide a more friendly atmosphere and it is easier to pour out your heart and share feelings with a group who knows you and respects your beliefs."

JOHN, age 16

Contemporary youth ministry makes heavy use of small groups. We use them for a wide variety of reasons. We can also use them for intentional spiritual growth. There are a lot of different models available:

Covenant Discipleship Groups

Covenant Discipleship Groups, and other groups like them, agree to meet weekly and hold one another accountable for their spiritual disciplines. They agree together to read the Bible, pray, attend worship, and participate in a variety of spiritual disciplines. The Upper Room has materials available for setting up and running such groups.

Spiritual Growth Groups

Spiritual Growth Groups are similar to Covenant Discipleship Groups, but are more flexible. The focus in a spiritual growth group will be less on holding one another accountable for specific spiritual disciplines, and more on giving one another support with the question, "How goes it with your spirit?" Some spiritual growth groups may resemble discussion groups and work through a book together. Others may resemble Bible study groups. Some will be more of a spiritual-support group and deal with personal agenda and issues, and their effect on our spiritual walk.

Sharing Groups

Sharing groups are support groups that deal specifically with personal emotional issues. But these groups lend themselves readily to spiritual growth concerns. A sharing group made up of church members and meeting at the church will include, as one of its natural components, the spiritual lives of the members. *Sharing Groups in Youth Ministry*, one of the books in Abingdon's Essentials for Christian Youth series is a complete handbook for forming and leading these groups.

Trips and Retreats

Trips, camps, and retreats provide the "mountain-top experiences" of youth ministry. While our relationship with God cannot be limited to these experiences, they can play a crucial role in adolescent faith. If given the choice between having a young person in Sunday school for six months or having the same youth in a camp for a week, many of us would choose the camp experience. It is that powerful and life transforming.

As youth workers, it is important that we both encourage our youth to participate in these experiences and provide the opportunity to debrief the experiences. The United Methodist Church, as well as most other denominations, provides high-quality spiritual-growth experiences at camps and retreats. Making sure that our youth are involved in these adds a whole dimension that we alone cannot provide.

I personally work in a large church with nearly four hundred active young people. We have a complex sophisticated program that provides many wonderful opportunities for these young people. But our conference and district camps, retreats, and events provide experiences for the youth of our church that we cannot provide. Kids come back from camp fired up and spiritually alive. I know that the whole spiritual tone of our youth group is changed by one of these events.

Debriefing these experiences is crucial. The kids have the emotional experience, but we need to help them make sense of the experience and translate what it means in terms of their life back at home, at school, and at church.

A SPIRITUAL LIFE RETREAT

I had an opportunity to go through a nine-month spiritual-formation program sponsored by Perkins School of Theology in Dallas, Texas. Near the end of that period, I was part of a design team for a spiritual life retreat for youth. This gave me an opportunity to incorporate many of the ideas and techniques gleaned from the course and its readings, and apply them to a weekend retreat for junior- and senior-high youth.

This retreat model has been widely used by a number of people in a variety of situations. It is included here as a model which incorporates many of the ideas suggested in this book, and one that can be readily adapted to a variety of settings. The retreat was built around the following elements:

* Small groups
* Journaling
* Praying
* Bible study (experiential)
* Fasting
* Meditation (experiential)
* Worship
* Spiritual growth gathering

The following material, containing the daily schedule and a detailed description of the retreat activities, is the leader's guide for the retreat. Each student's booklet should include several blank sheets of paper and copies of the following pages of the leader's guide: "My Spiritual Autobiography," and all four prayer-journal assignments.

Retreat Schedule

FRIDAY

7:00 P.M.	Registration
8:00 P.M.	Orientation

8:10 P.M.	Crowd breakers
8:45 P.M.	Community experience
9:00 P.M.	Spiritual family session
10:45 P.M.	Break
11:30 P.M.	Worship
Midnight	In rooms
1:15 A.M.	Bed check and lights out

SATURDAY

8:00 A.M.	Breakfast
8:45 A.M.	Worship
9:15 A.M.	Solitude
10:00 A.M.	Community experience
10:30 A.M.	Spiritual family session
12:30 P.M.	Lunch
1:15 P.M.	Recreation
3:00 P.M.	Worship
3:30 P.M.	Solitude
4:30 P.M.	Free time
6:00 P.M.	Supper
6:30 P.M.	Community experience
7:00 P.M.	Spiritual family session
9:00 P.M.	Dance
11:45 P.M.	End dance
Midnight	In rooms
1:00 A.M.	Bed check and lights out

SUNDAY

8:00 A.M.	Breakfast
9:00 A.M.	Solitude
9:30 A.M.	Community experience
10:00 A.M.	Spiritual family session
11:00 A.M.	Solitude
11:30 A.M.	Closing worship

Following is a detailed description of the retreat schedule:

Friday Evening

Theme: Is Something Missing?

Registration (1 hour)

Assign rooms; distribute pencils and student booklets. Organize activities such as volleyball, Frisbee, hikes, etc.

Orientation (10 minutes)

Welcome all the students to the retreat. Briefly review the rules, schedule, and student booklets.

Crowd Breakers (35 minutes)

Offer a time for the group members to get acquainted. Begin by singing lively, high energy songs. Then involve the members in group-building activities that enable them to get to know one another. It is especially helpful if you can get them into the small groups they will be in for the weekend.

An example of a crowd breaker: Divide into small groups of six to eight students. Ask the small groups to form circles. Have each person share:

1. His or her name.
2. One bit of personal information that no one else knows.
3. Something he or she has found that has helped him or her feel closer to God in the past.
4. A word or image that describes each person's relationship with God right now.
5. Why he or she came this weekend and what he or she hopes to receive.

Go around the circle once for each of the questions. This will give the group members time to think about their answers and keep the sharing moving without focusing too much or too little on anyone.

In this manner, you begin at a comfortable, nonthreatening pace, and then move the group members toward sharing and talking openly about their relationships with God. This kind of sharing may be new and difficult for some of your group members.

You're trying to set the tone for your group for the rest of the sessions, so keep the group moving toward sharing without pushing too hard.

Opening Community Experience

Guided Fantasy (15 minutes)

Ask some of the group members to read aloud John 1:1-5; 8:14, 16-18.

Explain that you will be taking them on a guided fantasy, based on these verses. Ask them to relax, close their eyes, listen, and imagine, as you guide them. Slowly say the following:

God is the creator and source of all that is. God is your creator. God gave you the gift of life. Experience the preciousness and sacredness of that gift . . . God has been present all your life. In some ways, you have known that and responded. Think of a time when you felt close to God . . . Feel God's joy and love at that moment . . . In many ways, we have missed that presence. We've not known God—not accepted God. Think of a time when you felt cut off from God—distant and alone. Feel God's sadness at the moment . . . .

God is here with you now—in the world, in your life. You can come to know God—experience God's presence in a way you never dreamed possible . . . God offers you grace—power to become what God wishes. Fantasize what your relationship with God could be . . . What is God's wish for you? How do you feel?

Spiritual Family Session

Writing Spiritual Autobiographies (15 minutes)

To move toward a deeper level of sharing, have the group members take 10 to 15 minutes to write a spiritual autobiography—a history of their relationship with God.

Ask the students to open their booklets to "My Spiritual Autobiography" (see below). Explain that they are to focus on their faith journey—their relationship with God as best as they are aware of it—and what has helped or hindered that relationship. The autobiographies don't have to be in complete sentences. The students are to strive for insights and notes on each of the eight areas on the worksheet. In addition, they are to think of anything else that has had an effect on their spiritual journey. The real object of this assignment is to give them material to share. Call time at the end of 15 minutes, even if the members are not finished. It is important to have plenty of time for sharing. Members can fill in verbally what they did not have time to write.

Sharing Spiritual Autobiographies (1 hour)

Ask each person to share his or her spiritual autobiography. Facilitate the discussion by going first, then asking for volunteers. After each person shares, open the group for questions and comments. Be alert for times when one member's story touches the other members' stories. Continue the process until everyone has had an opportunity to share.

After hearing all the stories, initiate a discussion on insights or comments on the autobiographies as a whole.

If you have a group that shares easily, use time in the second session to finish this exercise.

Introducing the Idea of Spiritual Growth (15 minutes)

In this exercise, you'll begin teaching about spiritual growth and introduce the concept of spiritual disciplines. Present the following in your own words:

* Spiritual growth is based on the idea that you can grow closer in your relationship with God and can become closer to God than you now are.

* For centuries, Christians have used specific tools to develop and grow in their relationship with God. These are called spiritual disciplines or spiritual exercises. These spiritual disciplines can be paralleled with other disciplines you are familiar with—athletics, music, or study—in any area of life in which you want to grow and become stronger.

* The idea of spiritual growth and spiritual disciplines may be new to some of you, but you already are familiar with many of the disciplines. We have just used two: guided fantasy using scripture and group sharing.

* How many other spiritual disciplines can you come up with? Some ideas include prayer, meditation, fasting, Bible study, confession, worship, journaling, solitude, service, and guidance.

We will be using and experiencing all of these—and more—this weekend.
Are there any questions?

My Spiritual Autobiography

Follow the eight steps below to trace your spiritual journey—the history of your relationship with God. You only have a few minutes, so don't worry about writing complete sentences. Just get enough down on paper so that you can share your faith journey with the other members of your group. Feel free to use anything that came to mind during the guided fantasy. Write down anything you think is relevant, but be sure to include the following items:

1. My earliest memory or awareness of God _____

_____

2. The major religious events or experiences in my life (family, church, youth group, camp, etc.)

_____

_____

3. My spiritual high point (time when I felt closest to God) _____

_____

4. My spiritual low point (time when I felt most distant from God) _____

_____

5. Special people who have played a role in my faith journey _____

_____

_____

6. Where I am right now in my relationship with God _____

_____

7. Where I would like to be in my relationship with God _____

_____

8. What's missing in my relationship with God _____

_____

Prayer Journal Assignment (5 minutes)

Introduce the idea of a prayer journal: a diary of one's relationship with God and one's spiritual life. Underscore the importance of solitude—a time to be alone with God away from all distractions. Explain that during the periods of solitude, they can focus their attention on God through the use of prayer journals.

Explain that during the journaling time, they will be able to think about their relationship with God, pray to God (on paper), and, most important, begin to listen to God.

Say that the journal assignments will be an important part of the weekend. Inform them that the results of the exercises will be shared in the small-group sessions.

Ask the students to turn in their booklets to "Prayer Journal—Assignment One" (see below).

Read aloud the definition of a prayer journal, as it is written on the page. Have the youth work alone on this assignment.

Closing Prayer Circle (10 minutes)

Ask the group members to stand in a circle with their arms around each other. Beginning with the person on your right, ask each person to say a prayer remembering the needs, pains, and joys heard from the person on their right, during the session. Go around the circle and ask each youth to participate.

Close the prayer yourself. Then lead the group in the prayer of Saint Frances by lining it out—you say each line, and the group repeats after you.

The Prayer of St. Francis

Lord,
    make me an instrument of your peace
    where there is hatred, let me sow love;
    where there is injury, pardon;
    where there is doubt, faith;
    where there is sadness, joy.

O Divine Master,
    grant that I may not so much seek
    to be consoled as to console,
    to be understood, as to understand,
    to be loved as to love; for
    it is in giving that we receive,
    it is in pardoning that we are pardoned,
    and it is in dying that we are born to eternal life.
    Amen.

End with a group hug, followed by individual hugs.

Break (45 minutes)

Prayer Journal—Assignment One

1. What is a "prayer journal"? Read the following descriptions of a prayer journal:

A journal is a personal record of feelings, thoughts, concerns, and visions, often written as a letter to God. Journal writing is a way of capturing the inner person to gain self-understanding. It includes any and every part of life, but is more concerned with meaning than with events, especially ultimate meaning.

All writing is just talking, put on paper. Many times we are not sure what we think until we say it. This is where a journal comes in. It is a safe place to face the parts of ourselves that we don't share anywhere else.

Writing in a journal or keeping a journal is a method that facilitates my taking time and effort to be honest with myself before God.

Writing in my journal is a prayer form for me. Prayer becomes attention to presence—not only God's, but our own . . . . The transcendent, which we so neglect and for which we have such deep yearning, is not only where God lives, but where we live when we are most alive.

Is there anything in those statements that stands out and speaks to you personally? If there is, write it below. Then make some notes about why this is important you.

_____

_____

_____

If anything is unclear, make a note so that you can bring it up in your next Spiritual Family Session.

_____

_____

2. Write a letter to God. Review your spiritual autobiography; focus on the parts in which you shared where you are now in your relationship with God, where you would like to be, and what's missing in that relationship. Add what you hope you can get here this weekend. Talk to God about what you discovered as you did your autobiography and reviewed the questions. Talk to God as you would to any close friend:

Dear Lord,

3. Have a conversation with Jesus. Read the following conversation with Jesus, written by Louise Spiker in *No Instant Grapes in God's Vineyard* (Judson Press, 1982), p. 56.

Me: My trust level isn't very high. I want signs, like the Old Testament people.

Jesus: Now, Louise, I want to help. What exactly is troubling you? Tell me about it.

Me: I'm not sure. I don't feel as okay as I want . . . I want to feel good, feel close to you, to feel some assurance that I'm on the right track. I'm tense and beginning to get a headache, but I came to the shore to get in touch with you and find peace and power (maybe) and direction. I don't know, Jesus, I just feel all mixed up.

Jesus: You're okay, Louise. You don't have to be perfect. You don't have to "arrive" at any certain place. It's okay to be where you are now. I love you, Louise. I love and accept you here, now, always. Rest in my love, Louise.

Me: Thank you, Jesus. I want to do that. How about if I just relax here on the beach and feel the sun as your love penetrating to the innermost parts of me?

Jesus: I think that's a good idea, Louise. Try it.

Go back and reread your letter to God. Write a dialogue (like the one above) in which you share your biggest concern in the letter and have Jesus respond. If you experience difficulty having Jesus respond, take a few moments of silence and see if some reply comes—something that Jesus or God might say.

Me:

Jesus:

Me:

Jesus:

Me:

Jesus:

4. Read John 3:1-21. Read the passage again and place yourself in the story. You become Nicodemus. You have the conversation with Jesus. Journal on the back of this page what you hear Jesus saying to you. Write a dialogue with Jesus, if you wish. When you've finished, close with a silent prayer.

Worship (30 minutes)

Open with a song. Build the worship around the scriptures used during the last session and the theme, "Is Something Missing?" Ask one or two students to share their spiritual autobiographies and what they learned from the experience. Allow one or two others to share insights from the guided fantasy. Close with a song.

"On spiritual life retreats, you get to leave the real world behind. Only those who are really involved in the church go, and there are less distractions during services. Retreats are a place where you can start new friendships and renew old ones. You can be yourself. Without your real world disguise, you are open to God's love and his plan for you."

KEITHEN, age 16

Saturday Morning

Theme: Listening to God Through Devotional Bible Study

Breakfast (45 minutes)

Worship (30 minutes)

Open with a song. Explore the idea of solitude: being alone, listening to God. Tell the students they will have an opportunity for 45 minutes of solitude after the worship. Say that they can work on their prayer journal assignment or just listen and relax. Close with the song "Humble Yourself."

Solitude (45 minutes)

Ask the retreat members to go off for a time alone to watch nature, pray, read scripture, and spend some quiet time alone. The materials they are to use are found in Prayer Journal—Assignment One.

Community Experience (30 minutes)

When everyone returns from their solitude time, take the group through the following experience.

Relaxation Exercises

Use exercises such as toe touches, stretches, and deep breathing.

Guided Fantasy

Lead the youth on a guided fantasy based on John 3:1-21. Retell the Nicodemus story. Ask the youth to imagine they are Nicodemus. Slowly read the following material:

"I am Nicodemus; I seek Jesus out by night. Why am I seeking Jesus? What questions do I have of him? What am I looking for? Why come by night? Who do I not want to see me? Am I ashamed? embarrassed?

I meet Jesus. What does he look like? Does he welcome me? What do I feel in his presence?

Jesus makes a puzzling statement, "Unless you change, you cannot enter my kingdom." Born again? How? That's impossible. Why does he say this to me? What is he really trying to say? What do I need to change in my life? How should I be different?

Jesus talks about two kinds of life. What in my life is worldly? What in my life is spiritual? How can I believe in what I've not seen?

God loves me so much, he sent his Son. For me? What is Jesus offering me? What am I missing? What is God telling me? How can Jesus make a difference in my life?"

Spiritual Family Session (2 hours)

Share Reactions

Discuss the guided fantasy. You've just come out of an experience that was new for many of your group members. Begin your Spiritual Family Session by inviting the group members to share their experience, feelings, insights, and reactions to the fantasy.

What was it like? weird? nice? Explain.

Have the group members compare the experience to the way they normally use the Bible. What's the difference? Which do they prefer? Do they usually read the Bible with the expectation that God will actually "speak" to them? Is that a new idea for anyone? What do they think about reading the Bible in this way?

Explain that a guided fantasy is one form of a "devotional Bible study"—reading the Bible in such a way that you expect God to speak to you personally through the story.

Tell your group members that they are going to experience another guided fantasy, one in which Jesus would offer them something that could change their lives.

Guided Fantasy

Ask three young people to read John 4:1-26; 6:26-27, 34-35. Invite the group members to get comfortable, either in their chairs or on the floor.

Read the following meditation slowly. Feel free to change or adapt it as you wish. Use the ellipses (. . .) for pauses to let your group members' imaginations go to work.

"Feel yourself falling . . . falling back through time . . . farther . . . to a far distant land long ago . . . You're thirsty . . . You go over to the water bucket for a drink . . . but it's empty . . . You decide to go down to the well outside town and get some water and bring it back . . . You leave your home . . . step out into the street . . . feel the heat . . . hear the sounds of animals . . . which ones can you hear? . . . Can you see them? . . . You can smell someone cooking lunch . . . What are they cooking? . . . What is someone arguing about? . . . You're now outside town, headed for

the well . . . You hear birds singing . . . It's so hot . . . You're thirsty . . . You look up, and there is someone sitting at the well . . . a stranger . . . He looks tired . . . and thirsty . . . He's . . . Jewish! . . . Your people and his people have hated each other for centuries . . . Feel the anger inside . . . Is he dangerous? . . . Do you feel fear? . . . He doesn't look dangerous . . . You know he hates you . . . All Jews hate your people, they always have . . . He's saying something to you . . . He wants you to get him a bucket of water . . . You have a bucket and he doesn't . . . 'What! You, a Jew, ask me, a Samaritan, for a drink?' . . . Before you realize it, those words have slipped out . . . Strange, he doesn't seem mad, he's smiling . . . Now he's speaking to you again . . . 'If you only knew what God is offering you right now, you'd be asking me for a drink . . . a drink of what I can offer you . . . a drink of living water' . . . You find yourself wondering, 'What's water got to do with God' . . . God is offering me something right now? . . . What is living water? . . . And who is this guy . . . talking about 'living water' and doesn't even have his own bucket . . . He's speaking again . . . 'Whoever drinks from this well will get thirsty again, but anyone who drinks what I have to give will never be thirsty again . . . What I have to give is eternal life' . . . What kind of water is that? . . . To never be thirsty again . . . To never feel empty (and at times I feel so empty) . . . To be satisfied . . . at peace . . . You hear yourself asking for some of this special water . . . He starts speaking to you again . . . You can't believe what you're hearing! . . . He knows! . . . Your deepest, darkest secret . . . He knows!!! . . . How? . . . How does he know that! . . . Who is this man? . . . Is he some kind of prophet? . . . He's speaking to you again . . . 'You worship God one way, and I worship God another . . . I worship the God I know, you worship a God you've never really known . . . never really experienced . . . never really loved' . . . How does he know these things about me? . . . He's still speaking . . . 'The time will come, in fact is here now, when you will no longer worship God the way you have in the past . . . No, from now on you will worship him in spirit . . . and in truth' . . . You find yourself praying . . . 'Oh, God, I wish it were true . . . Can I really feel close to you . . . can I be close to you?' . . . Who is this man? . . . 'Your Christ will come . . . We all look forward to that day when we can really know God and feel close to God' . . . He speaks to you again . . . 'I, who am speaking to you, whoever comes to me will never be hungry. Whoever believes in me will never thirst' . . . You look into his eyes . . . You know the hunger in your life . . . the emptiness . . . You know what you thirst for . . . and he is offering it to you . . . right now . . . (long pause) . . ."

"Take a moment to bring yourself back into this gathering. When you are ready, come back to our group circle."

Discuss Guided Fantasy

Initiate a group discussion on the experience. Focus on some of the following questions:

* How did the use of the five senses at the beginning help you get into the story, make it more real?
* What was it like to place yourself in the story?
* What was it like to meet Jesus?
* Could you clearly identify your deepest, darkest secret? What is it like to think Jesus knows even that about you?
* What does "living water" mean to you? What do you think God is offering now, here this weekend? Are you beginning to get an idea of what you can get in your relationship with God that you didn't have?

Discuss First Prayer Journal

Ask the youth if they understand a "prayer journal." Did the descriptions they were given in the first session help? What do they think about the idea of a prayer journal? Have any of the group members journaled in the past? If so, have them explain.

Were the group members able to write a letter to God? Was it difficult to do this? Explain. Ask if anyone will share his or her letter. Break the ice by sharing your own letter.

Probe to find how the group felt about moving beyond writing a letter to God to actually entering into a conversation with God. What was that like? What's it like to think of God "speaking" to you? Does it feel awkward to "listen" to God?

Would anyone be willing to share his or her "conversation"? You can facilitate this by going first in sharing your dialogue.

Go Over Second Prayer Journal Assignment

Go over the second assignment for the prayer journal (see below). Ask if there are any questions.

Closing Prayer

Stand in a circle. Ask for favorite songs, then sing one or two. Go around the circle in prayer, with each member lifting up the concerns, joys, or sorrows that other members shared during the session. Close the prayer yourself. End with a group hug and individual hugs.

Lunch (1 hour)

Saturday Afternoon

Recreation

This is an intense weekend for many youth. Use the time after lunch as a recreational time so that the retreat participants can unwind and drain off pent-up energy.

Worship

Open with a song. Build the service on the scripture used in the session, and the theme "Listening to God Through Devotional Bible Study." Allow a few participants to share reactions to the guided fantasy and the first prayer journal assignment. Close with a song.

Solitude

Ask group members to complete Journal Assignment Two.

Free Time

Supper

Prayer Journal—Assignment Two

1. Take a few moments to center yourself—experience solitude, enjoy being alone. When you're ready, do the following exercise.

2. Read John 2:13-16. Read the passage over again, using each of your senses. If you had been there, what would you have seen? heard? smelled? felt? tasted? Place yourself in the story. Where would you have been? Who would you have been? What would you have felt? done? Journal the results of your meditations below.

_____

_____

_____

Use the Temple as an image for your life. What is there that shouldn't be? What clutters up your life and keeps you from what's really important? What in your life do you think would really offend Jesus? Identify as many things as possible and use the space below to journal them.

_____

_____

_____

3. Journal a prayer to God. Lift up the clutter you see that keeps you from having the kind of relationship with God you would like to have.
Dear Lord,

4. Concentrate. Close your eyes, center yourself, and mentally go over what you've written. Use a period of silence to see if you can "hear" God speak to you about what bothers you. If that's difficult, try journaling a conversation with God about the clutter in your life.

Me:

Jesus:

Me:

Jesus:

Me:

Jesus:

Me:

Jesus:

5. Offer a silent prayer.

Saturday Evening

Theme: Listening to God Through Prayer

Breathing Exercise

Lead the group in slow, deep breathing. Have the group try and "breath scripture": "Be still (inhale) and know (exhale) that I (inhale) am God (exhale)."

Broadening Traditional Forms of Prayer

Introduce the following traditional forms of prayer and allow time for the students to imagine . . .

* *Praise and thanksgiving:* Feel God's love, God's joy . . . Give thanks to God for . . .

* *Confession and pardon:* Measure your life by what God would like you to be . . . Where are disappointments? Feel God's sadness . . . Lift these to the Lord . . . Receive God's forgiveness . . . Feel God's forgiveness enter you . . . Imagine God hugging you . . . Imagine love flowing through your veins . . .

* *Petition:* Ask for God's help in some area of your life . . . Imagine God's love embracing you without words . . . Feel God's strength and power flowing into you . . . Feel your problem growing smaller, God's power growing stronger . . .

* *Intercession:* Think of someone in your group or at home who has a problem. Ask God's help for that person . . . Image God's love embracing him or her . . . Image God's power and strength flowing into that person . . . Image his or her problem or pain growing weaker as the power of God grows . . .

New Ways to Pray

Introduce the following new ways to pray. Allow time for the students to imagine . . .

* *Centering prayer:* Focus on the center of your body . . . Release tension, be at peace . . . Feel peace flow out from your center . . .

* *Emptying prayer* (kenosis—one form of contemplation): Relax, release tension . . . Remove everything from awareness . . . Be empty, silent . . . Dwell in empty silence . . . Listen to silence . . . Listen to God . . .

* *Jesus prayer:* "Lord Jesus, have mercy upon me, a sinner" . . . repeat this over and over in your mind . . . See if any word stands out, if any images or thoughts come . . . Let your imagination go . . . Go with whatever comes into your mind . . .

* *Mantra:* Lift up one word in your mind, such as *life, love, peace, joy* . . . Repeat the word over and over in your mind . . . Begin to feel what the word means . . . Feel *life, love, peace, joy* . . . Dwell in the feeling . . . Let it flow over you . . . into you . . . through you . . .

Spiritual Family Session

Discuss Reactions to Exercises

Begin the session by asking the group members to share their experiences and reactions to the prayer exercises. Incorporate the following questions:

Which of the exercises were new to you? Which did you find difficult to get into? Which did you enjoy or find difficult to get into? Which did you enjoy or find particularly helpful? Explain. Which was the most vivid or powerful? How does this way of praying compare with the way you usually pray? What do you think about this approach? Which of these could you use in your own prayer life? Share your reactions, thoughts, or feelings about prayer as listening to God rather than telling God something.

The Importance of Listening

Ask the group to discuss what it takes to make a good friend. What do they look for in a good friendship? What does it take to maintain a good friendship?

Once the group has a good idea of what friendship is and what it needs, ask what the group thinks about the following three qualities in a friendship:
* *time together*
* *quality time (away from all distractions)*
* *listening*

Ask the group members to think about their relationship with God as an intimate friendship. Ask what they can lift up from the discussion on friendship and apply to their relationship with God. Do we nurture our friendship with God? Do we take time with God? Do we have quality time away from all distractions? Do we ever listen to God, really expecting that God can speak to us? What kind of clutter do we allow to get in the way of our friendship with God?

Discuss Second Prayer Journal Assignment

Have the group members share their journaling experiences. Were they able to use the devotional Bible study techniques to make the scripture more real? What happened when they placed themselves in the story? What "clutter" were they able to identify? (What gets in the way of their friendship with God?) Could they identify anything they feel might offend Jesus?

Cleansing the Temple

Explain that one of the primary goals of the spiritual disciplines is to create a place in our lives where God can speak to us, to remove all the clutter—all the conflicting claims on our time and our energy—so that we make room and time to be with God.

Four of the spiritual disciplines are specifically intended to remove clutter—the noises and distractions that keep us from listening to God. As you go over these four disciplines below, the idea is to find if any of these could be useful in getting rid of some of the distracting clutter that we have identified. (The goal is to initiate sharing and discussion.)

* **Solitude.** Share the following definition of solitude with the group:

Solitude, as a spiritual discipline, means to spend time alone, in silence, listening to God. It is deliberate stepping back from all the activities, people, distractions, and noise of our normal day, so that we can spend some quality time with God.

Your group has now had two opportunities for solitude this weekend. Ask the group members to share what those experiences were like.

Ask if anyone experiences solitude at home—being totally alone, in silence (no stereo, radio, or television). What's that experience like at home? Could the experience be negative (lonely)?

What regular times of solitude would add to your relationship with God that is not already there? What clutter might it remove?

* Fasting. Ask what fasting means. Then share the following definition:

Fasting, a spiritual discipline, means to abstain from food for a set period of time for spiritual purposes—not to lose weight or to make a political point (as in a hunger strike). The spiritual purpose of fasting is to heighten awareness of God's presence and free us from a preoccupation with food.

To better understand how fasting can heighten awareness, ask if they have ever eaten so much that they became sleepy or sluggish. Explain that not eating, especially for a long period of time, can do the opposite—it can make a person more alert and aware.

Ask if anyone in the group has ever fasted. If so, discuss the experience. Encourage the group to ask questions of those who have fasted.

If no one in the group has fasted, you might share some of the following information:

Those who do fast say that it can make us more alert and aware of things around us and with us, including God's presence. People who fast find that after 24 to 48 hours of fasting, it is much easier to pray. Fasting also can free us from a preoccupation with good. Most of us spend a good amount of our time eating, talking about food, preparing food, or thinking about food. It consumes a lot of our time and energy. Many people are surprised to discover that they don't need to eat three times a day. After a day or so, the person who is fasting may not even be hungry, and may even find his or her energy level has increased.

Initiate a discussion on fasting. What are fears and myths about fasting? Is it a spiritual discipline the youth might like to try?

* Simplicity. Read the following quotation from *Celebration of Discipline: Paths to Spiritual Growth*, by Richard Foster:

Simplicity is freedom. . . . Because we lack a divine Center our need for security has led us into an insane attachment to things. We must clearly understand that the lust for affluence in contemporary society is psychotic. It is completely psychotic because it has completely lost touch with reality. We crave things we neither need nor enjoy. We buy things we do not want to impress people we do not like. . . . We are made to feel ashamed to wear clothes or drive cars until they are worn out. The mass media have convinced us that to be out of step with fashion is to be out of step with reality.

Ask whether Foster is overstating the case. Is happiness to be found in more and more "things"? If we have enough, own enough, possess enough, if there is enough money in our bank account, will we be happy? Get the group to think bout this for a few minutes.

As a spiritual discipline, simplicity affirms that more "things" cannot make us happy; in fact, possessions can clutter up our lives and lead us away from what's really important. In our society, many believe that the importance or worth of a person is measured by the wealth or the amount of possessions. The discipline of simplicity says that this is not true.

Ask if the group can identify ways in which the "lust for affluence" makes relationship with other people and with God more difficult. Do they experience this in their school? churches? families? Where else?

How could this discipline help their personal relationship with God? What clutter could it remove from their lives?

* **Submission.** Read the following definition of submission:

> Another word for submission is *servanthood*. As a spiritual discipline, submission affirms that the way to self-fulfillment is through self-denial—to hold others' interests above one's self-interest.

Initiate a discussion on this definition. Is the idea offensive? naive?

After everyone has had an opportunity to react to the definition, ask if anyone has ever encountered a person who seemed totally absorbed with himself or herself. Have them discuss their reactions.

Have the youth ever known someone who seemed to value them as much as they valued themselves? If they have, have them discuss their reactions. If not, have them fantasize what it might be like to know such a person.

Encourage the youth to consider the idea of a group—like your group—in which all the members are more concerned about one another than about themselves.

How could the discipline of submission help their relationship with God? What clutter could it help remove?

Go Over Prayer Journal Assignment Three

Ask the students to turn to the third prayer journal assignment (see below). Ask if there are any questions.

Closing Prayer

Stand in a prayer circle. Sing a song such as "We Are the Family of God." Go around the circle in a prayer, having each member lift the concerns heard during the session. Close the prayer yourself. End with a group hug and individual hugs.

Dance

All group members should be in their rooms by midnight, with lights out at 1 A.M. If a dance is not appropriate for your group, you might want to schedule an informal fellowship time, such as an afterglow or some other activity that allows the youth to get to know each other better and process their feelings about the weekend.

Sunday Morning

Theme: Listening to God Within "The Body"

Breakfast, Pack, Load (1 hour)

Solitude (30 minutes)

Ask group members to complete Prayer Journal Assignment Three.

Prayer Journal—Assignment Three

1. How has God come to you through other people? How have people been important in your faith journey? Go back to your autobiography. Who has helped you? Name specific people, events, and experiences. What was it about these persons that made them instruments of God in your life? Were they special in any way? Journal what you uncover.

_____

_____

2. Review the weekend so far. Who has God used for you this weekend? How has God used them? Do you think God has used you this weekend to help anyone else? Write your answers in the space below.

_____

_____

3. Read I Corinthians 12:12-30. How has God used "the body" (the church, your youth group, camp, individual Christians) in your life?

_____

_____

How has God used you to help others?

_____

_____

4. Write a prayer letter to God. Lift up what you've discovered during this assignment.

Dear Lord,

5. Close with a silent prayer.

Community Experience

Relaxation and Guided Fantasy

Ask the group members to lie on the floor so that each one is both supporting and supported by others. Slowly read John 15:1-8. Take them on a guided fantasy:

"Imagine yourself as the branch. You are drawing nourishment and strength from God (the vine) . . . Feel the strength flowing in . . . flowing into your feet . . . up through your body . . . out of your arms and head . . . flowing into you, through you, to others around you . . . You're being supported by other branches around you . . . by the bodies you are lying on . . . You are not alone . . . You are surrounded, supported . . . Feel that support . . . Feel strength, nourishment flowing into you from those around you . . . Feel the connection between you and everyone else here . . . all a part of the vine . . . God's strength flowing into you from others . . . flowing to others from you. . . ."

Ask the youth to keep their eyes closed as you read First Corinthians 12:12-30. Then take them on a second guided fantasy.

"Imagine yourself as one small part of a body . . . Feel the other parts of the body around you . . . so small, dependent on the other parts . . . for nourishment . . . for help . . . for life . . . You can't say to others, 'I don't need you' . . . Cut off from others, you would die . . . so small, yet important . . . You have your part to do . . . Without you the work would not get done . . . Feel the others who rest on you . . . depend on you for support . . . No one can say to you, 'I don't need you' . . . Without you the body would not be whole . . . Feel a sense of belonging . . . You are a part of the body . . . Feel your place, how you are connected to all around you. . . ."

Spiritual Family Session

Discussion

Ask the group to process the two guided fantasies.

* **The Vine:** What was it like to be a part of the vine: Could you feel the strength flowing into you? Does that ever really happen to you? Explain. What was it like to feel yourself supported by others? Where do you get that in real life? at home? in school? at church? in youth group? here? Have you ever felt cut off from the vine and other branches? What was that like? How important is being a part of the vine to you personally? Could you be more attached than you are, more supported?

* **The Body:** Compare "the body" exercise with "the vine" exercise. How were they different? similar? What's it like to have to depend on others? What's it like to have others depend on you? Are you needed? important? Do you have a contribution to make?

Discuss Prayer Journal Assignment

Ask the group members to share how God has come to them in other people in the past. Guided the sharing with the following questions: What did these people do? How are these people different from others? Do you think God has ever used you in someone else's life? Has God worked through anyone this weekend? (Use these questions to set up the next exercise.)

Spiritual Healing Exercise

Ask the group members to sit in a circle on the floor. Ask for a volunteer. The volunteer is to share one hurt or need he or she has. The rest of the group is to try to listen and understand that hurt. The youth cannot give advice or try to "solve" the problem. They can ask questions to try to understand the problem better, and they can share their concerns. When the person feels the group has heard and understands his or her problem, he or she should lie down in the middle of the circle while everyone else places one hand on him or her. Each person in the group then gives a verbal prayer for the person in the center. The prayer lifts up the pain or problem and asks for healing. When the prayer is finished, have the person in the center share what the experience was like for them. Repeat the process with other volunteers.

Prayer Journal Assignment

Ask the students to turn in their booklets to the fourth prayer journal assignment (see below). Ask if there are any questions.

Closing Prayer

Have the group get into a circle and begin with a song such as "Jesus My Lord."

Join in a prayer circle, giving thanks for the weekend. Close the prayer yourself, and lead the group in the Lord's Prayer. Close with a group hug and individual hugs.

Solitude

Give the group time to complete the fourth Prayer Journal Assignment before they go to worship.

Closing Worship (30 minutes).

Open with a song. Build the service on any scripture used the past weekend and the theme "Spiritual Growth—Reaching Out." Allow time for the students to reach out to the two people they identified in their fourth prayer journal assignment. Close with several of the songs that were sung during the retreat.

Prayer Journal—Assignment Four

1. Read John 21:15-17.

Identify someone in your church youth group who needs help and support; be very specific. What does the person need?

_____

_____

_____

Identify someone at the retreat (who is not in your group) who needs help and support.

_____

_____

_____

Write how you can help meet this need before you leave today. Be aware that you will be given an opportunity to reach out to these two people during the closing worship service.

_____

_____

_____

2. Review the weekend—all you have learned and experienced. In the space below, write what you will take home with you from this weekend, to use in your spiritual journey. Note any commitments you've made.

_____

_____

_____

SELECTED RESOURCES

Bible

Teaching the Bible to Adults and Youth, Dick Murray (Nashville: Abingdon Press, 1993).

Dreams and Spiritual Growth

Dreams and Spiritual Growth: A Christian Approach to Dreamwork, Louis M. Savary et al. (Mahwah, N.J.: Paulist Press, 1984).

Prayer

Celebration of Discipline: Paths to Spiritual Growth, Richard J. Foster (New York: Harper & Row, 1980).
Explorations in Meditation and Contemplation, Harvey Seifert (Nashville: The Upper Room, 1981).
No Instant Grapes in God's Vineyard, Louise Spiker (Valley Forge, Penna. Judson Press, 1982).
Opening to God: Guided Imagery Meditation on Scripture, Carolyn Stahl (Nashville: The Upper Room, 1977).

Spiritual Growth

Feeding Your Forgotten Soul: Spiritual Growth for Youth Workers, Paul Borthwick (Grand Rapids: Zondervan Youth Specialties 1990).
The Ministry of Nurture: Helping Teenagers to Grow Spiritually, Duffy Robbins (Grand Rapids: Zondervan Youth Specialties, 1990).
Spiritual Growth in Youth Ministry, David Stone (Loveland, Col.: Group Publishing, 1985).

Worship

Creative Worship, Faye Schwartz & David Mohr (Loveland, Col.: Group Publishing, 1992).
Creative Worship in Youth Ministry, Dennis C. Benson (Loveland, Col.: Group Publishing, 1985).
Introduction to Christian Worship, James F. White (Nashville: Abingdon Press, 1990).